TEACHING DISPLAYS

Teaching
Displays

Their purpose, construction, and use

by Mona Garvey

LINNET BOOKS
1972

LIBRARY OF CONGRESS CATALOGING IN PUBLICATION DATA

Garvey, Mona.
    Teaching displays.

      1. Teaching—Aids and devices. 2. Visual aids.
      3. Bulletin boards. I. Title.
LB1043.5.G3   371.33'5   72-270
ISBN 0-208-01286-9

photographs and displays by the author

© 1969, 1972 by Mona Garvey
Published 1972 as a Linnet Book
by The Shoe String Press, Inc.
Hamden, Connecticut
All rights reserved
Printed in the United States of America

CONTENTS

INTRODUCTION

Bulletin boards and displays can be the nemesis of many teachers. Most teachers accept, at least in theory, the premise that displays of some kind are necessary in classrooms. Many are somewhat hazy as to exactly why this should be done, but the fact that display areas are provided indicates that one is expected to make use of them. An additional complication is the prevailing belief that displays require artistic ability and a certain knack which one either has or does not have. This belief has probably been perpetuated because it is comforting to our artistic inadequacies, but it is false. Artistic ability is undoubtedly useful, but it is not at all essential to the preparation of effective displays. What is essential in the absence of such talent is the development of a new attitude toward displays based on a few principles and learnable skills.

Unfortunately our education has provided many of us with neither the proper attitude nor the principles and skills for the job. Few education courses do more than mention the subject in passing, and it is not until entering your own classroom for the first time that you fully realize that those empty bulletin boards are your responsibility. One's first impulse is probably to simply cover the space with whatever comes to hand, but one's second impulse is, or should be, to find out how to *use* the space rather than merely cover it over.

The most obvious sources of help are the many display books on the market and the many dozens of pamphlets. Most of these materials fall into four main types:

- Materials dealing with specialized areas of display work such as lettering and construction techniques; skills involved are often complex for the beginner but are useful in extending one's display proficiency
- Materials presenting step-by-step breakdowns of professionally prepared displays; seeing how professionals do it helps to generate ideas and to establish desirable standards
- Materials centered around actual classroom displays; discussions of teacher-made displays serve as idea sources on both teaching and display techniques
- Materials dealing with sketches of proposed displays with suggestions for materials to be used and for layouts.

These four types of materials are all good idea sources but it is seldom advisable to copy any of the illustrated displays in toto: your display area may be a different shape, color, or texture from the one shown; the materials you have available may be a different size and shape; and the display may not suit your students or your teaching unit. If you do wish to copy a display, be highly selective in your choice; an unskilled amateur cannot duplicate professional work, and displays done by fellow amateurs may be poor educationally and artistically (inclusion in a display book or pamphlet is no guarantee of quality). It is far better practice to adapt the ideas of others to the materials and space you have available, to your clientele, to your teaching objectives, and to your own abilities. In order to do this, however, you must learn some of the principles and skills involved in creating displays.

Unless one is extremely talented, it is impossible to learn how to paint by looking at a masterpiece, to play a concerto by listening to a recording, or to execute a display by looking at a completed product. Therefore this book will teach display techniques by using display mock-ups. This book uses no professional displays, no sketches, and no classroom displays. It does use actual display components or simulated components (such as blocks of paper to represent student reports or other printed matter) to show possible arrangements of materials. None of the sample displays is intended to be copied. The intent is to use the sample display and display components to teach you how to do displays of your own. Once you have mastered a few rather simple display techniques you should be equipped to select display ideas from other sources and then adapt them to fit your requirements.

This book will consider the theoretical aspects of display work (elements and principles of design and forms of displays); discuss practical considerations (design backgrounds and layout); and "teach" necessary art skills (lettering and cartooning). It will also offer suggestions on design shortcuts (use of reusable design and cartoon components) indicate sources of display ideas, and furnish technical information.

It is impossible, however, to consider the "how" without the "why" and in the educational field the "why" is the sine qua non of the whole endeavor. Consideration will be given to the "why" of audiovisuals in education, and, more specifically, to the whys and whens of displays in education. Displays will be presented in the educational framework in which they will be used and suggestions will be made for displays which will introduce units, help in their development, act as a cumulative activity, and indicate further areas of study.

It is well to keep in mind that no one book, pamphlet, or article will solve all display problems. The skills which you have, the skills which you lack, and the situation in which you are working are all unique; there can be no one source or general approach designed to your exact specifications. For this reason you should consult a variety of sources to collect the bits and pieces to add to your skills, smooth over your non-skills, and help you to do your job more easily and effectively. This is no easy task but if one has to do displays or supervise their execution, it is a professional responsibility to do it well. It is hoped that this book will help you to do it better.

I wish to thank the H.W. Wilson Company for permission to use as Chapter V of this book a chapter from my book, *Library Displays,* which it published in 1969. This discussion of design is as pertinent to teachers as it is to librarians.

TEACHING DISPLAYS

I

AUDIOVISUALS IN EDUCATION

educational contributions of audiovisual materials
and specific goals and methods for use of displays

Teaching displays have been around for a long time—probably almost as long as man himself. The cave men often relied on pictures to communicate feelings and ideas; their first pictures were probably scratched into dirt with a pointed stick, but others were painted on cave walls. We have no way of knowing exactly why these cave paintings were done but there are theories. Some anthropologists believe that drawings and paintings of animals were done as a kind of magic to inspire hunters and to provide insurance for a successful hunt; others theorize that the paintings were executed as a record of a hunt.

The paintings may have been done for either of these reasons, and, if so, they meet some of the recommended uses of teaching aids in the classrooms of today; to introduce a subject, to teach something about it, and to summarize a learning experience. They also magnificently fulfill one of the important auxillary requirements of a successful visual display—to help create an attractive and stimulating learning environment. As the first recorded visual aids in history, the cave paintings were undoubtedly an outstanding success.

3

The special concern of this book is with the visual part of audiovisuals, and, to narrow it down even further, to non-projected visuals. It is important, however, to begin with an overview of the whole range of audiovisual materials in order to see how the display materials fit in, and, even more important, to see how all of the audiovisuals fit into the total teaching situation.

This skimming of some of the principles involved in the use of these teaching aids will, of necessity, be brief, but the purpose is to provide a background for the discussion of the whys and wherefores of displays in schools. Too many books treat school displays as problems of decoration rather than of education, but no school display—however decorative—is effective unless it is tied to valid educational goals. Decoration is important and a pleasant environment does contribute to learning, but decoration is a secondary function of displays and education is the primary one.

Classroom bulletin boards and displays have long been important educationally (even though they have not always been treated as such), but today they are receiving more attention as part of the whole range of non-book teaching materials. The advent of more sophisticated teaching machinery and the plethora of new teaching materials have directed ever more attention to the place of audiovisual materials in teaching. *Audiovisual* (or AV) is a general term with no really accurate definition and other terms are used for the same kinds of things: teaching materials, teaching aids, teaching tools, and instructional or curriculum materials. The problem in selecting and defining one general term is due to the wide range of materials to which the term refers; the most sophisticated programmed teaching package and the simplest teacher-made graph are both training aids—or AVs. Whatever they are called, they are evidently here to stay.

Some of the earlier advocates of programmed teaching predicted that specialized audiovisual materials would eventually make teachers obsolete; follow-up studies, however, have indicated that teaching aids will remain aids and that teachers will remain teachers. Therefore, since both audiovisuals and teachers seem to be fixtures in education, an effort must be made not merely to maintain an uneasy truce but to form a creative partnership. The producers of audiovisual materials are making a greater effort to offer materials that will fit in with current teaching methods and to suggest ways the teacher can integrate the materials into the subject units. There are still a few holdouts within the teaching profession, but most teachers are at least acquiescent (and more and more are becoming enthusiastic) about the classroom influx of audiovisual materials.

Fortunately the many books on the use of audiovisuals in the classroom are helping to forge a strong partnership by presenting technical information in simplified terms, by discussing teaching techniques necessary for the effective use of audiovisual materials, and, perhaps most important of all, by emphasizing the role of the teacher and of the solid teaching techniques involved. It is very important for teachers to realize that while some of the techniques may require the polishing of old skills and the acquisition of new ones, the chief requirement is still creative teaching. Audiovisuals are useful aids, but the teacher's methods and skills are the controlling factors in the effectiveness of any teaching aid.

Each audiovisual specialist has a favorite list of values derived from use of audiovisual materials in an educational situation. These lists vary in emphasis and point of view, but among the often mentioned values are that audiovisuals make learning more interesting, help to make it more permanent, extend the boundaries of experience, provide a common basis of experience, and stimulate individual action. Any time there are values to be derived there are recommended guidelines for their attainment. Some of the suggested steps are that the teacher prepare himself, the students, and the environment; present the materials; and then follow up. Each of these steps is in accord with sound teaching methods and each is the responsibility of the teacher; the actual use of the audiovisual material is only one part of the learning process in which it is involved.

There are also guidelines in the selection of materials to be used, and the choice depends on the subject matter which is being taught, the background and level of the students, the availability of materials, and the teacher's adeptness at using the materials. The third and fourth factors are the stumbling blocks for many teachers. Some teachers will use any materials related to the subject regardless of the level and the production quality of the materials, or despite his own lack of skill with the type of materials selected. The excuse is that this is the only thing available and that the student will get "something" out of it. Unfortunately the "something" may be negative. Materials which are of inferior quality, inappropriate level, or which are poorly presented can turn students off educationally. If suitable commercial materials are not available, the teacher should seek out or make audiovisuals to meet the needs of the teaching situation. And a teacher must, of course, learn to use the materials effectively.

All of these general goals and guidelines apply to displays, and many of them will be discussed later in relation to specific types of displays. Display materials of course have some values and guidelines of their own. In her book *Display for Learning,*† Marjorie East lists some of the goals of displays:

1. Concentrate interest and attention
2. Show the basic structure of an idea
3. Explain abstract terms by relating them to concrete things
4. Bring scattered ideas together to form new concepts
5. Turn ideas into words
6. Encourage expression.

Since there are specific goals to be achieved with displays, there are, of necessity, suggested methods of achieving them.

†Marjorie East. *Display for Learning: Making and Using Visual Materials* (New York: Holt, Rinehart & Winston, 1952).

6

The first step is to establish the educational purpose of the display and the purpose or purposes should be stated—at least mentally. The second step is to visualize the display—to simplify the idea and to translate it into graphic form. The third step is to decide what materials will be used in presenting the display and whether they will be teacher-, student-, or professionally prepared materials, or a combination of different materials. The fourth step is to determine the type of display best suited to the idea and to the available materials— whether the idea would be conveyed best by a sign, a poster, a bulletin board display, or an exhibit. The fifth step is to execute the display according to design principles, and the final step is to evaluate the display in terms of the goals achieved and the materials used.

Each of these steps, regardless of the order in which it comes, is essential in the creation of an effective display. In theory the purpose of the display comes first and the other steps are taken in order. In practice, however, the sequence may be entirely different. For instance, the teacher may have to design the display to fit a particular display space instead of choosing the goal of the display and then selecting the appropriate space. There will also be times when a teacher will wish to display student projects or photographs, drawings, or other material related to a unit of study. In this event a teacher should try to relate the materials to some unifying theme and to establish a definite educational goal.

These guidelines in the preparation of displays are concerned chiefly with the direct educational functions of displays. There are secondary educational functions (such as the learning that takes place when a student helps prepare display materials) and there are social and aesthetic functions to be served. These functions are overlapping and most displays can and should contribute to all three. This may seem a heavy load of responsibility to heap on one display, but the functions do fit together easily; a carefully designed bulletin board display, for example, may serve as an introduction to a unit of study (educational goal), it may contribute to an attractive room atmosphere (aesthetic function), and it may contribute to the social interaction of the group (especially if student work or ideas are used in preparing the display).

These functions will be separated for the purpose of discussion, as will consideration of types of displays, design principles and elements, and many of the artistic skills necessary to do the job well. These discussion divisions will be somewhat arbitrary, but it should be kept in mind that all of the seemingly disparate pieces will be fit back together again in Chapter XI.

II

DIRECT EDUCATIONAL FUNCTIONS OF DISPLAYS

display methods of introducing, developing,
summarizing, and extending study units

As has already been mentioned, displays can serve different functions and the most important of these is educational. There are both direct and indirect educational functions of displays but the direct function is considered first.

The direct educational function operates in four ways: to introduce a subject or procedure which will be taught, to help explain a subject, to summarize a learning experience, and to suggest related areas of study. Displays used to introduce a new subject or unit of study usually require the greatest amount of ingenuity and salesmanship. Enough information should be provided to pique the student's curiosity without frightening him with the complexity of the subject; nothing untrue should be promised or implied (never hint that a new math unit will be easy and fun, or that a home economics course will make someone an expert cook or seamstress). The abilities and the interests of the students should be kept in mind when selecting and arranging the display materials.

Introduction

One introductory technique is to display work done by a previous class, and it is often possible to make assignments with this possibility in mind. Students can be told that the best projects will be kept for use in displays—if they are durable and conform to certain size specifications which will make them easy to store and display. Another possibility is to select some of the best projects and have the students redo them with better display materials: maps and drawings might be redrawn with marking pens on poster board, science projects might be remounted on a durable and attractive background such as burlap-covered fiberboard, and materials executed on flimsy paper could be mounted on poster board in a contrasting color. It is often advisable for any labels to be redone in larger sizes, and, for display purposes, they are best done with marking pens on blocks of white poster board. Students are usually willing to redo projects, but, if the projects are to be retained by the teacher, the raw materials—the poster board, marking pens, fiberboard, and so forth—should be provided by the school.

If the subject introduction is to involve a procedure, as might occur in various arts and crafts classes, it is often possible to show a finished project and then to show some of the steps involved in producing the work. It is not usually practical to show a finished table and then to have three other tables depicting various stages of completion. But a finished table might be displayed in connection with a bulletin board which shows, on small blocks of wood, how the table finish was executed; or the bulletin board display might show, again using blocks of wood, how the legs and the top of the table were joined. It is also possible to use one sample project to demonstrate different stages of development. For instance, a carved leather project such as a billfold can be divided into four strips showing the tracing of the design, the carved design, the tooled design, and then the design as it looks dyed and waxed. Another possibility is to present different methods of doing the same thing: different methods of sewing a seam, making a wood joint, taking a photograph, applying paint, writing a poem, or running a football play.

These two methods of introducing procedures, showing stages of development and different approaches, are very effective introduction techniques; unfortunately both require considerable preplanning and time. It must be decided which steps or approaches will be most effective to "show" and easiest for the student to comprehend; it then must be determined how the samples will be executed, how they will be displayed, and how they will be labeled. It might be possible to have a student prepare the samples, but, if this is done, the samples should be executed according to the teacher's specifications, and the final display should be done or carefully supervised by the teacher. This type of display is time consuming but it is well worth the effort since the basic display materials can be used over and over again in different arrangements and for different purposes.

True and false, matching, and multiple choice quizzes are often very effective for introductory displays and they can be used for almost any subject. Shakespeare can be introduced with a quiz listing quotations or characters (either well known or obscure depending on the student level) to be matched with the play from which they come; groups of authors can be matched with titles, characters, or selections from their works; scientists can be matched with discoveries, artists with paintings or styles, musicians with compositions; and, of course, any individual can be matched with dates of birth and death, profession, and country of origin. The same technique can be used for social studies by matching well-known landmarks with cities, or countries with geographical features; a history unit might be introduced with a quiz matching events with dates, countries, or famous individuals involved in the events; science experiments can be matched with what they are to prove or disprove.

Multiple choice questions can be used with science experiments (this test proves A, B, or C); and they can be used with answers to math problems, with procedures (A, B, or C should be done first), or with identification of plant or mineral samples. Multiple choice is also good with almost any kind of verbal or language test; one might ask for synonyms or antonyms of words relevant to future units of study; definition of foreign words, perhaps using foreign words similar to English words, could be used as an approach to the study of a foreign language or country; and sentence completion might be used to introduce materials, equipment, or procedures which will be studied. True and false questions are very adaptable and can be used with any subject; they might, for instance, ask about health or safety, people, events, cause and effect situations, organizations, or techniques.

Most subjects lend themselves to all three types of quizzes, and one need only choose the preferred type and select appropriate questions. It was mentioned before that introductory displays should not intimidate students; quiz questions, therefore, must be carefully chosen. Difficult or tricky questions might be best with advanced students, but beginning or slower students should be attracted with at least a few rather simple questions. The questions are, after all, a preview of coming attractions rather than a test of learning. One good way to point this up is to include a few questions just for fun. A matching quiz on composers might include a popular composer and one of his latest hits, and a quiz on famous quotations and who said them could include, "Never trust anyone over thirty."

Two of the type quizzes we have been discussing are shown in figures 1 and 2; both quizzes are mounted on fiberboard which has been covered with natural burlap. Figure 1 uses a basic cartoon figure holding a toothbrush, a caption done with green poster paint letters outlined with a black marking pen, and four blocks of text done with marking pen writing on white poster board. Other than the caption, the only color is supplied by a wide strip of green construction paper and green numbers glued to squares of white paper (the numbers are used more for design than anything else). This particular introductory quiz may be used from the middle grades to the

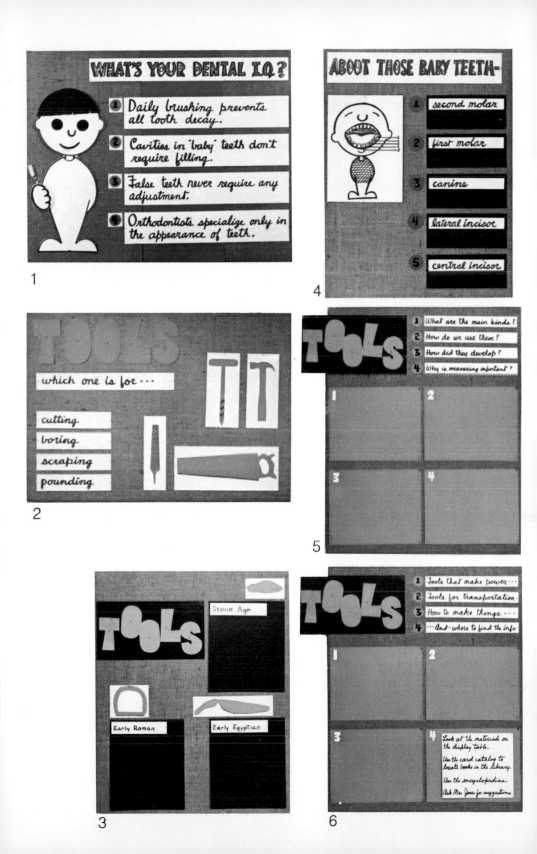

1

WHAT'S YOUR DENTAL I.Q.?

1. Daily brushing prevents all tooth decay.
2. Cavities in "baby" teeth don't require filling.
3. False teeth never require any adjustment.
4. Orthodontists specialize only in the appearance of teeth.

4

ABOUT THOSE BABY TEETH—

1. second molar
2. first molar
3. canine
4. lateral incisor
5. central incisor

2

TOOLS

which one is for...

cutting
boring
scraping
pounding

5

TOOLS

1. What are the main kinds?
2. How do we use them?
3. How did they develop?
4. Why is measuring important?

1
2
3
4

3

TOOLS

Stone Age

Early Roman

Early Egyptian

6

TOOLS

1. Tools that make power...
2. Tools for transportation
3. How to make things...
4. ...And—where to find the info

1
2
3
4. Look at the materials on the display table.

Use the card catalog to locate books in the library.

Use the encyclopedias.

Ask Mrs. Jones for suggestions.

parent range since the answers are not as elementary as they might seem. The answers may be posted nearby, they may be found in dental care pamphlets being distributed, or they may be ascertained by attending the PTA meeting on child health care.

Figure 2 is a matching quiz introducing the concept that tools are designed for different, specific purposes, and that these tools fall into four main groups. The caption letters are of green construction paper, the tools of the same paper mounted on poster board blocks. For purposes of unity, two of the tool blocks are the same size, and a third is the same length as the other two; also note the even margins along the sides and bottom of the display. The components in both of these displays are simple and easily executed (even by students), and, since all are separate pieces attached with map tacks, all are rearrangeable and reusable.

Each of these introductory techniques is designed primarily with the educational function in mind. Even though the display might not *teach* anything about the coming subject, it should give some indication of the scope of the material to be covered (work done by a previous class will indicate this to some extent); suggest some of the techniques involved (such as wood finishing or wood joining); relate the subject to previously learned material (quizzes matching people with their professions or with events); or relate the subject to something particularly relevant to students (a math percentage quiz involving batting or fielding averages of baseball stars). The display is not intended to offer complete information about any aspect of the subject or any procedure involved; it is intended only to give an indication of what is involved, and, hopefully, to make the student eager to know more.

Explanation

A second direct educational function of displays is explanation of a subject. These training aids also can show step-by-step procedures or differing techniques, but, since the material will be immediately relevant in the classroom, more

13

specific details can be included in a display used as a teaching aid than in an introductory display. This type of display can serve as a reference aid for both teacher and students; the teacher can refer to it while making explanations and the students can refer to it later for reinforcement of the learning experience. A reference aid display might include anatomical drawings, cross sections of plants, diagrams of football or basketball plays, drawings of architectural features, outline shapes of implements used in a certain field, or art reproductions. These supplementary teaching aids are often shown to students by use of films, slides, transparencies, or projected drawings; or some of them might be drawn on the chalk board. All of these are valid and useful techniques, but some of the materials should be on view—to refer to and discuss—for a longer time than these techniques make possible. This can be accomplished by using some of the materials available in transient forms as the basis for displays; these displays are intended to reinforce, not to replace, the other teaching techniques.

In addition to drawings, pictures, diagrams, and cutouts, a reference aid display might include formulas, recipes, discriptions and characteristics, samples, difinitions, and basic dates and facts about people, places, or events. A teaching aid display might also be set up in outline form. Used in this way it will give an indication of the amount of material to be covered and the order in which it will come. Another possibility is to fill in the outline as the study progresses; points can be added as they are covered and the display will serve as a day-by-day record of subject development. A compromise system is also possible, and, in this case, the main points of the outline would be listed in advance and the details would be added as they are covered. This cumulative approach is an excellent way of helping the student visualize and synthesize what he has learned.

Figures 3 and 4 show two different display layouts which can be used for explanatory displays. In figure 3 the board is divided into three areas with large pieces of black poster board; three cutouts of early cutting tools are used (construction paper mounted on poster board); student-lettered captions (marking pen on poster board) and green cutout letters are map tacked to the black poster board. This particular display is somewhat small if a number of student reports are to be added, but the same layout may be used on a larger board. The teacher-made tool cutouts may be replaced by student drawings or cutouts as the unit develops.

Figure 4 is a prototype of an explanatory display board which has already been partially filled in. One might begin with just the caption, cartoon, and numbered blocks. The tooth name may be added as it is discussed in class—or the names could be mixed up on the display, and then sorted out in the proper place as they are discussed. The next step might be to add explanatory written or typed information under the name of the tooth. Here too you might wish to use a larger display board and provide larger background blocks for more information or for student work.

Summation

A summation type of display can be assembled in a number of different ways, and many of the approaches are similar to the introductory and explanation type of displays. Quizzes can be used to test knowledge of what has been learned, and outline or step-by-step displays can also help summarize the learning process. These displays will be more effective if students suggest some of the quiz questions or supply the projects or materials to be used. If the unit involves individual or group projects, these can form the basis of a culminating exhibit; all of the projects can be displayed or only the best can be selected. Sometimes a combination of the two approaches can be used; all the projects can be shown for a short period of time, and then the best projects can be used to make a carefully constructed and designed exhibit or bulletin board display.

Student-collected materials can be the basis of a display. If the items are small—plants or leaves, rock samples, shells, photographs, drawings—they might be mounted on uniform size pieces of black poster board. All the materials should be labeled and this should be supervised by the teacher. The labels should be of uniform size, and, with younger students, the teacher should determine the wording and help students mark guide lines to keep the lettering of fairly uniform size. The teacher should make the selection of materials to be included in the display and should also decide on the final arrangement of the materials.

In many cases teachers leave the assembling of a summation display entirely to the students, but, as a rule, this is not advisable. Working on a cumulative project is a valuable educational activity for students, but selection of salient materials and their logical and effective arrangement are often beyond student capabilities. Students should contribute as many of the display materials as possible, and they might "rough in" the final display arrangement. The teacher, however, should see that the materials are of good display quality (drawings may need to be larger or mounted on poster board, and labels may require rewording), supervise the logical arrangement of materials, and assist students in coordinating elements into an effective design. The teacher and students should discuss display criteria, evaluate the finished display, and decide how future displays might be improved. The amount of teacher assistance required will depend on the competence and initiative of the students and the complexity of the display problem.

An example of a coordinated teacher-student summation display is shown in figure 5. In this case the teacher would design the layout and decide on the questions which will direct attention to some of the learning objectives of the unit. The students might then prepare and select the materials to be displayed. Greater coordination would be achieved if the teacher and students together decided on the questions which would best reflect the goals of the unit. The green background areas will provide maximum contrast with student reports on white paper, and the very stable layout will hold its "shape" even if the display materials are scattered around in each area. The cutout numbers are a directional and design device. This technique, incidentally (numbered headings in one area corresponding with numbered areas elsewhere) can be used to coordinate a number of display boards relating to one subject. Numbered headings can all be placed on one board, and then matching numbers and related materials on other boards—the board with the headings functions as a table of contents.

A similar display layout is shown in figure 6. The captions here, however, indicate areas of interest not studied during the unit. Information displayed might come from students in the class who have done extra research, or from other classes which have studied this related material. Another possibility is to use study prints or photocopies of pictures and articles related to these areas. In this display the area numbered 4 lists sources of added information, but one might also list specific book titles or subject headings under each area of interest. But now we have progressed into another educational function which is—

Related Study

The fourth educational function, as we saw in figure 6, can utilize many of the approaches discussed previously. The purpose of this type of display is to motivate and point the way toward related studies; this might include areas of study which are too advanced for many of the students, or which are peripheral to the main subject of study—or areas which there was not time to cover in detail. To be most effective, this kind of display should not only motivate students toward related studies, but should offer some directives to anyone who might be interested; one might include lists of related books or, as in figure 6, indicate where additional information can be located.

All of these educational functions—introduction of a subject, explanation, summation, and suggestion of additional areas of study—are a standard part of teaching technique. In too many cases, however, these techniques are either not applied, or are haphazardly applied, to classroom displays. Many teachers, with no artistic aptitude and no training in display techniques, can spend hours on a display which turns out badly and has little if any educational value. These teachers justifiably feel that their time and effort could have been better used elsewhere. This is true, but perhaps the time and effort expended in making bad displays might be better invested in an effort to acquire a few basic display skills and techniques. Once some basic skills are learned, each display will produce more effective results with less time and effort. Effective displays can be of tremendous value to both teachers and students, and learning to design them is a useful and necessary part of a teacher's education.

III

SECONDARY FUNCTIONS
OF DISPLAYS

indirect teaching functions; social functions;
aesthetic functions

The direct educational function usually concerns one teacher communicating to one group of students. There will be times, however, when a teaching display will be directed toward other students, faculty members, school administrators, board members, parents, or the general public. The expected audience is an important factor in the planning of a display, and a display designed expressly for any of the above groups will differ from a display planned for the members of one's class. It should be kept in mind, however, that a display designed for one audience will also be seen by, and have an effect on, secondary audiences.

Displays done for (by, or with) one group of students will be seen and judged by other students. Students like to know what is happening in other classes and displays are often their only contact with activities of another class. If the displays are dull and unimaginative, a negative impression will be formed. If, on the other hand, the displays are attractive and stimulating, students may be excited about attending that particular class or studying the same subject in their own classroom. Since we are all sensitive to the approval of disapproval of our peers, the success or failure of class displays may have a decided effect on class morale.

Teachers also depend on classroom displays for information on activities in other classes and in other schools. Teachers learn from other teachers and displays are effective communication channels from one teacher to another. When a teacher visits another classroom his impression is based, in part, on the appearance of the room—not just the physical appearance but the "educational" appearance. Displays are a reflection of teaching techniques and class activities, and if exciting things are happening in the classroom they should show up in the displays. Even if the classroom teacher is not present, a visitor can often discover new ideas, materials, and techniques for use with his own students. If he has an opportunity to talk with the teacher responsible for the display, it may serve as an entree to discussing how the subject materials were presented, how assignments were made and evaluated, what educational goals were sought, and how successfully they were achieved. This kind of discussion can and does take place at any time, but the presence of visual teaching materials makes a discussion of techniques more relevant—and that is one of the purposes of using visual aids.

Good classroom displays are of considerable value to student teachers and substitute teachers. A teacher entering an unfamiliar classroom situation is in a difficult position and classroom displays can be useful props in getting things moving. Students can be asked to explain and discuss some of the display materials and to relate then to the unit being studied. This discussion of the display offers the teacher an opportunity to evaluate the class and to get a better grasp of the subject matter, how it is being approached, and how far the study has progressed. This can be particularly valuable when the lesson plan is sketchy or when the teacher is unfamiliar with the level and educational background of the students.

This provision for a visual review lesson not only helps the substitute to get oriented, but helps the regular teacher by assuring that unit study will progress in his absence.

Administrative duties make if difficult for school superintendents and principals to visit classrooms as often as they might wish; when they do have an opportunity for a classroom visit they must absorb as much as possible in a brief time. Since it is difficult to explain or understand learning activities which are not observed over a period of time, effective displays provide important capsule, visual records of class activities. The teacher can use the display to show and tell what is being studied and how it is being presented, and the administrator can refer to the display when asking about specific problems and progress of the students—whether the students worked well together in assembling an exhibit or how they researched maps and drawings on display.

If an administrator visits when class is not in session, the displays may provide his only clue to current activities and special projects. An administrator knows the progression of study units at various grade levels, and a good display should enable him to determine the unit being studied and how it is being presented. This is especially important when he is showing visitors through the school. Instead of saying just "This is the third grade" he can use the displays to explain what the third grade is studying—even though he may not have known what was being studied before entering the classroom. Being able to present this type of on the spot information has obvious advantages for the administrator himself, the visitors, and for the classroom teacher who makes the display available.

Since parents do not know the policies, procedures, and techniques of teaching, they are at a particular disadvantage when they enter a classroom. They are further handicapped by the "how we were taught" syndrome and lack of exposure to newer teaching methods. Their children are no help either. Papers and projects which children take home give only a slight indication of classroom activity, and the children are notoriously poor at explaining what they "do" in school. The burden of explanation is on the teacher, and displays combined with the aforementioned show and tell technique can help the teacher bridge the communication gap.

Displays can assist a teacher in pointing out teaching methods and goals by furnishing a starting point for discussion, offering a frame of reference, and providing a pleasant educational atmosphere. A teacher can use a display of student reports to point out approaches to reading and self-expression; a social science display might explain why geography is no longer a separate subject; and a history display might clarify why cause and effect concepts are more important than memorizing dates and events. General discussion of this type is not only informative but can help a teacher ease an uneasy parent or disarm a contentious one. It can also serve as a natural introduction to discussing the work and progress of an individual student—the main reason for the parent's presence.

When it comes to lack of familiarity with modern teaching theory and methods, members of the school board or board of trustees are sometimes in the same situation as parents; unfortunately they are often reluctant to admit their lack of expertise. Adept use of classroom displays can help educate board members without directing attention to possible gaps in their knowledge. An administrator or teacher may, for example, use a display to show how a particular concept (visualization of an abstract idea) is presented to students. This visual explanation provides a foundation for more knowledgeable exchange of ideas between faculty and board members.

All of these secondary educational functions—effect on other students, teachers, administrators, parents, and board members—depend on the same display made for classroom use. Whether the response is favorable or not depends on the effectiveness of the display. A display which is well designed from both an educational and aesthetic point of view activates a positive response which reflects credit on the teacher, the

22

class, and the school. If, on the other hand, the display is haphazard educationally and artistically, the reaction will be negative. This kind of instant judgment is sometimes unfair to a teacher but we all react to what we see, and it is part of a teacher's responsibility to make the "seeing" in his classroom a positive experience.

Displays can also serve important social functions; they can affect student-student, student-teacher, and student-school relations. As visual records of learning experiences and class activities, displays contribute to the self-esteem of individuals in the class and to the group as a whole. There is a "look what we've done" sense of proprietorship about an exciting bulletin board exhibit, and, if students have contributed to the display, this pride is heightened. Preparation of class displays offers students opportunities to make individual contributions to the class and to work together with other students; this opportunity is especially important if a child does not perform well in regular class work or in casual social situations.

An added benefit is the opportunity to work with a teacher on a different basis than is possible during regular classwork. A student may have more design know-how than a teacher and the display might involve a student's special interest or hobby. This temporary shift of control can provide both student and teacher with new insights; a student may find that a teacher is human and a teacher may discover in the student abilities of which he had been unaware.

Students tend to feel that school administrators are not concerned with their interests or problems, and that policy decisions are made without considering them. Displays cannot solve this communication problem, but, since displays are communications channels, they can be used to help alleviate the situation. Displays devoted to student interests and opinions can encourage students to present their viewpoints in coherent, constructive, and creative ways. Assignments can be made for bulletin board displays presenting student policy suggestions or showing pro and con sides of school policies and regulations. Administration can do its part by evaluating the display viewpoints and by seing to it that effective displays of this type receive outside-the-class exposure.

Displays can promote a different sort of social contribution by providing a "look and discuss" area in the classroom. There are always a few loners or new students who need a semi-social meeting area in the classroom; a bulletin board and exhibit area can provide this. The presence of a display will not resolve any social problems, but it can offer a before and after class lingering area and a topic of discussion among students. It can also furnish an inconspicuous waiting space for a student who wishes to talk to the teacher or to another student "accidentally." If Charlie Brown could have hung out around a bulletin board display, he might have had an opportunity to talk to the little red haired girl more than once a year. It is a small service in a class, but a valid one.

Aesthetic function is, technically, a secondary function of displays but it is one which should not be underestimated. Effective design is necessary for effective visual communication. A display may have an important message to deliver, but the message will not be transmitted clearly if the communication channel (in this case the design) is deficient. Design principles and art skills are methods to insure the clear transmission of your message; they aid in planning the format of the message, help clarify the transmission, and assure that attention will be paid.

The aesthetic function is important psychologically. Classroom decor permeates the whole learning environment, and the appearance of the classroom has important psychological effect on teacher and student. School planners strive to make classrooms both functional and attractive, but, however well they succeed, a room is impersonal until a teacher and students put up displays which reflect their interests and taste. Classroom displays should be attractive because students learn better in pleasant surroundings; they should be personal because it is "their" room; and they should expose students to good design which will help in the formation of their artistic taste. Displays should provide an educational, personal, aesthetic, and stimulating environment for teaching and learning.

IV

FORMS OF VISUAL PUBLICITY

educational use of signs, posters, bulletin boards,

and exhibits

In theory there are four different forms of visual publicity which serve different functions and require different approaches. The terms are overlapping and are used interchangeably so that it is sometimes difficult to determine where one stops and another starts. The four forms of visual publicity are signs, posters, bulletin boards, and displays and exhibits.

Signs

A sign is a lettered notice which is intended to advertise something or to give direction or warning, and it is probably one of the most abused and misused members of the publicity family. Signs all too often have been relegated to telling people not to do things, and, with the possible exception of supermarket and department store signs, they often do not tell us where to go or what to do in an unfamiliar situation.

In a classroom the teacher is usually dealing with one group of students at a time and most of the directions are oral. Some signs are necessary, however, to indicate the location of certain materials, to reinforce rules or procedures which have been dealt with orally, and to remind students to do or not do things. A sign offers no guarantee that a student will note or heed the information on it, but at least it gives the student an added nudge in the right direction. Signs are also helpful for new students who may not be familiar with class routines.

Classrooms should probably have more signs of the informational type than they do, but signs outside the classroom are the biggest problem in schools. The problem is that they usually are not there; if they are, there are too few of them to provide assistance. The "school" seems always to assume that anyone entering its portals should know where to go for whatever he wants. Not so. There are innumerable individuals, including new students and teachers, who enter a school requiring at least minimum directional signs. It is disconcerting to a visitor or newcomer to be wandering around a building in search of an individual or an office; it is also distracting to classes to have someone wandering the halls.

There should be signs at every school entrance indicating where a visitor is to present himself and telling him how to get there. When something special is in progress and the uninitiated are expected, adequate signs (accompanied by floor plans if at all possible) should be provided for. Once the student, teacher, or other visitor has been directed on his way some signs of assurance would be an added courtesy (This is the right line for registration; this is the room for fourth grade students; right this way for the teachers' meeting). Schools are such complex mazes that directional signs are important not only to a visitor but to the school; and a school's generosity—or lack of it—in providing signs will affect an individual's reaction to the school.

Permanent signs should not be cryptic notices taped here and there; they should be fresh and clean and should be replaced at the first sign of age. Signs in the same area should be the same size (unless the messages vary greatly in length) and they should be on the same color poster board and printed in the same type and size of lettering. Preferably each sign should be map tacked to a larger piece of painted or burlap covered fiberboard. They should not be affixed with transparent tape since that looks hasty and sloppy and it turns brown and old looking very quickly. Signs of special importance and interest can be made more attractive and effective if they are held by a cartoon figure or hand; or an arrow or asterisk may be used to direct attention to the signs.

Figure 7 shows three of the elements which have been mentioned: a basic sign, a floor plan, and a cartoon figure. The "1st grade registration, room 203" does provide basic information, but, unless one knows the location of room 203, the information is inadequate. If the small floorplan were then added beneath the sign, the "registrant" would not only know where to go but how to get there. Then if a cartoon figure and attractive background are added, the sign not only provides information and directions but is attention getting and good looking as well. Of course the sign is now on the verge of becoming a poster, but, as stated previously, these display forms tend to overlap.

Temporary signs should conform to some of the above rules. They should, if possible, be done on poster board and hurried signs should be written with a marking pen (quick amateur writing usually looks better than quick amateur printing); and it takes only a few extra seconds to avoid down-hill slope by ruling in some lettering guide lines. Reusable backgrounds (such as the cartoons and arrows mentioned above) would also be a good idea. All of this is part of the school's public relations and it should not be overlooked.

Posters

A poster is very much like a sign in that it gives brief information about something; the difference is that a poster is a pictorial design telling a brief story. A poster, like most signs, requires only a few moments of attention; the message is intended to be seen and absorbed quickly. A poster is usually concerned with only one point; it should be colorful and eye-catching with a clear and direct message; and the poster and text should be large enough to be seen at a distance. A poster may publicize an important event; advertise a specific product, service, or business; or incite the reader to some specific action.

Since posters deliver a very limited message, their use in the classroom is often limited to inciting the reader on matters relating to health, safety, and good citizenship. These are topics which can be covered in detail through discussion and use of other audiovisual aids, and making a poster about one aspect of a problem is usually not worth the teacher's time—though prepared posters might be used to complement other aids. Posters, however, present an interesting problem in the communication of ideas—how to simplify a complex idea and present it visually—and having students design posters related to class studies can be a challenging assignment.

Outside the classroom, posters are much in evidence around a school. Students often make posters to publicize activities such as sports events, dances, plays, band concerts, recitals, and so forth. Most of these poster activities are planned under the guidance of a teacher who may not be directly involved in poster making but who should be able to offer advice about design and execution. Therefore, even if a teacher does not make posters for his own classroom, he should know how to go about it.

Artistically a poster has to be simple and direct; there is usually space and "time" to convey only one idea and this must be done with economy of effort. In terms of color all that is needed is black and white and one color—or black *or* white and two colors. There should be one eye-catching shape or drawing, a very short caption, and a brief text. If details about a product, service, idea, or event are necessary they can be included, but the viewer should be able to get the general idea without reading details—he can refer back to them later if sufficient interest has been aroused.

If a number of posters are needed, it will probably be necessary to have them reproduced commercially, in which

7

8

9

10

case they will be flat and two dimensional. If, however, you are making your own posters, texture and depth may be introduced. There are a number of ways of doing this. One effective device is to include related pamphlets or flyers as part of the design. Construction paper pamphlet holders are easy to make and they can be glued or stapled to a piece of poster board which may, in turn, be attached to the poster (The holders could be attached directly to the poster, but if they are affixed indirectly they can easily be peeled off and reused). Pamphlet holders add an extra dimension to the poster; they can be a colorful and effective asset to the design; and, since the viewer is encouraged to touch a part of the poster, an attention-getting participation factor is added.

If the poster components (cartoon, caption, and text) are on separate pieces of poster board, it is quite easy to make some of the pieces project from the surface. Any light easily attached object will add dimension and interest, and textured materials and patterned fabrics may be used. Anything which adds dimension, texture, or movement will make the poster more interesting and will make it easier to deliver the message which the poster conveys.

An example of a very basic type poster with a caption, sub-caption, and pictorial design is shown in figure 8. The poster board background is in blue, and the caption is blue with a black outline. The poster is colorful even though only one color and white are used. In figure 9 the same components have been mounted on poster board, and four categories have been added to form the basis of a sequential display. Typed, written, or photocopy text about "bennies" may be posted under each category. The following week the asterisk can be moved to "snow", the caption beneath the figure changed to cocaine, and the text changed to provide information about it. But now that we have moved the poster components to a new environment and expanded the message, we are discussing a different type of display—a bulletin board.

Bulletin Boards

A bulletin board, technically, is a board on which notices and announcements are posted. A bulletin board is also a big problem to almost anyone having to use it. In many schools bulletin boards have been built in as part of the room decor and are of the wrong color and size and in the wrong place for display purposes; in some buildings they have been added as an afterthought and are tucked in corners or squeezed in on top of chalk boards. Therefore, before any decisions on form, function, or any artistic consideration can be made there is often a physical problem with which to cope.

The first step in dealing with the physical problem might be to measure all the boards and determine just how much usable space is available and how much unusable space should be adapted or disguised. It is often impossible to have existing boards removed—those we have to "do with" and some "do with" suggestions are offered elsewhere in the book—but it is often possible to have some boards added which are designed to our specifications. One of the best solutions is to make several moveable display setups which can be used in different locations in and outside the classroom.

Burlap-covered fiberboards are excellent for this purpose. They are easy to make, inexpensive, light; and, most important of all, attractive and adaptable. A 2 foot by 3 foot bulletin board of this type can be mounted on a wall, propped on the chalk board tray, or placed on an easel. Since burlap has a nappy surface it may be used as a flannel board. If the burlap is brushed, any materials backed with felt or flannel will stick to it—and materials used for a flannel board demonstration may then be map tacked to the board for a bulletin board display.

It has already been mentioned that a bulletin board is for the posting of notices. This is only one of the uses to which it can be put, but since it is one of the usual ones, and often the messiest one, it will be considered first. The most important thing to keep in mind about notice boards is that the materials, however temporary they may be, must be arranged according to some plan; they should not be tacked up helter skelter on the excuse that they will be there only a short time. The board should have a heading and/or cartoon, cutout, or some other attention getter; and if there are subdivisions of material, these should be set off in some way and should have a "lead" caption.

Notices should not be tacked directly to a bare board. The surface may be covered with a coat of paint, fabric, or construction paper backing (use with caution since it fades and must be changed often); the covering material should be of a texture and color which will provide maximum contrast with the notices. Since the whole board will seldom be changed at one time, there should be a durable display background to make the board more attractive, more effective, and more easily used in the arrangement of temporary materials.

In the classroom this type of board might be devoted to a class newspaper with students clipping items or writing and drawing original material to be used. This type of newspaper might deal with current events or record "on the scene" versions of historic events being studied in the class. This can be a very effective classroom activity since all of the students may participate and each of them may be editors, sports writers, columnists, cartoonists or whatever for a week or a month at a time. It is important for the teacher to see that the paper has a well-lettered masthead and captions and that the background is well designed—perhaps using different colored blocks of poster board for the various subject divisions.

Most notice boards in a school are located in hallways or in students' or teachers' lounges. Boards outside of classrooms may be "no mans land" (though *someone* should assume responsibility for all display space). They may be assigned to teachers or classes on a permanent or rotating basis; or the school clerks or student aids may get stuck with them. Whoever is in charge should decide exactly what is going to be done about them. The first thing to be done with notices is to determine the categories into which they fall—usual subjects, usual size and shape, length of time for which they are posted—and whether or not there are too many or too few to fill the space available.

After the notices have been grouped according to subject, size, and length of stay, it will be necessary to assign priorities and space. First priority for general boards might go to notices directly relevant to the school or to school events; second to general educational notices; third to activities of school connected organizations; and fourth to community and cultural events. Bulletin boards expressly for teachers will have different priorities, but the operating principles are the same—decide what type of information is most important and assign space accordingly.

Since school and educational notices have first priority (excluding notices of a permanent nature) they should occupy the most prominent space. If bulletin board space is limited, they should occupy only one board; if there are several entrance boards one should be saved for a large poster type display. In most school systems the posters and notices are usually a standard size; therefore the display background can be designed with this in mind. Provisions can be made to display notices side by side, or, if there are many notices, they might be arranged in layers or in overlapping "lift" patterns. If series of regular size notices are received, acetate covers could be permanently affixed to the board and the new notices slipped into the covers. Space for posters might be sectioned off and made more noticeable by means of a cartoon figure pointing to the space, or an all-purpose caption might be used.

If clippings are often displayed for short periods of time, a definite space should be designed for them. A cartoon figure holding his coat open could be used and clippings attached to the coat lining; a cartoon figure could be wearing a sandwich board to which notices could be attached; a cartoon hand might be holding a small notice board; or clippings could be displayed on a bright piece of poster board which is set off with a caption, arrow, or asterisk. (Incidentally all of the above devices are excellent space fillers on a too large display board).

The main thing to remember is that miscellaneous

34

clippings—especially if they are of different sizes—must be brought together in some definite arrangement or confined in some definite area. Once the background arrangement is set, the notices can be changed as often as necessary without disturbing it.

A second priority board might include materials relating to educational notices of various kinds; in a grade school this would include contests and awards of interest to students; in a high school to materials on colleges, scholarships, and training courses; and in a college or university to advanced study programs and jobs. Here too, the design of the board should not be disregarded just because the materials will be changed often; a background design should be planned and a caption and/or cartoon should be added. There might also be subheadings for divisions of materials, colorful pamphlet holders could be used to hold handout material.

Activities of school and community events should also be posted on carefully designed boards. If the boards are small, lift arrangements can be used. If the boards are too large for what is usually posted, there are various types of space filling designs which will alleviate the problem. Some space filling possibilities were suggested earlier in this chapter and others will be discussed and pictured in later chapters.

Permanent notices should not be displayed on the bulletin boards; it may be necessary to post them somewhere, but they are usually most unattractive and are of little immediate interest or use to most people. Depending on the number, size, and shape of permanent notices, they can either be kept together or posted where they will do the most good as messages and the least harm as displays. They might be mounted on attractive backings and posted near the most relevant area (the fire notice near the exit and the no smoking near the trash containers), or they might all be posted on some relatively obscure board headed "For the Record."

In addition to the notice posting function, a bulletin board may function as a large sign. This type of sign may be used for a holiday or special week, to call attention to a special event, or to honor someone connected with the community or with the school. This type of advertising might be presented in the form of a quiz; for example the school might have a series of one, two, or three question quizzes focusing on the history of the school, facts about the school or faculty, interesting information about graduates of the school, or just about anything which might be of interest. Any signboard ought to begin with a good design background, the sign should be large and effectively lettered, and each sign should be displayed for only a few days at a time—and if a quiz sign is used the answers should be posted nearby or under a lift panel on the same board.

A bulletin board may also serve as a poster, and, used in this way, is subject to all of the rules applying to posters. The chief advantages a bulletin board has over a regular poster are the usually larger size, the more prominent placement, and the fact that it is easier to use fabric, 3-D devices, and other objects on it. It is much easier to attach items such as pamphlet holders, lift panels, and small objects to a bulletin board than to a poster. This relative ease of attachment also means that bulletin boards can often be used for displays and exhibits of objects and three-dimensional materials.

Displays and Exhibits

Display and exhibit have similar meanings and both terms are used as both nouns and verbs. A further complication to pinning down the meanings is the fact that both words (especially display) are often used to refer to the whole range of nonprojected visual publicity. In practice, however, a display is usually a bit more limited in scope than an exhibit but there is no definite dividing line. In a narrower sense both terms refer to arranging objects in such a way that we see the object itself and also the connective idea that ties the individual items together; there has to be some theme or message behind the organization of the materials. The display or exhibit might show progression or growth, or aspects, views, or interpretations of a subject; and it may be limited to a particular medium or form, to a geographic area, to a period of time, to an individual or particular group of people, or to a subject of study.

If the materials are two dimensional or not too heavy, they might be displayed on one or several bulletin boards. Objects may be shown on shelves attached to the boards or suspended by wire or cord. Large displays, or displays involving both two- and three-dimensional items, might utilize bulletin boards and tables or display cases. A display or exhibit of any kind usually requires special arrangement in terms of gathering the materials, grouping them in a coherent manner, and arranging suitable space, and there is, in addition, the problem of making the display both attractive and effective educationally. The arrangement must be logical and clear; there must be sufficient labels with sufficient information; and design principles must be adhered to.

School displays and exhibits will usually be a cooperative venture on the part of the teacher and the students. The display materials will often be made or collected by the students and they may also print the captions and labels and arrange the materials. The teacher, however, should exercise some control over how the materials are arranged, captioned, and displayed. The arrangement should not be a hodgepodge assembling of diverse student projects. If the executing or gathering of materials was done according to some plan, this plan must be evident in the display of the materials. If projects were assigned with no definite theme in mind, then some sort of theme must be imposed on the materials.

If, for example, students bring in rock samples which are simply given identifying labels and lined up, that is not an exhibit. However if the rocks are divided into categories—and each category includes drawings or explanations of where the samples were found or how they were formed—that constitutes an organized exhibit. If the rocks are attractively displayed (perhaps on shelves backed with contrasting colored paper), labeled with a consistent lettering style on uniform size pieces of poster board, and with an effective lead caption—that constitutes an effective, organized exhibit.

Figure 10 is an example of an exhibit (or display) which meets most of the criteria which we have discussed. The rocks are divided into groups, and each type of rock has a short caption telling how it was formed. And the display of these materials is logically and carefully arranged; the captions and poster board shelves are all the same size and the arrangement is simple and attractive. A bit of added interest is provided by the brief quiz about the different rocks shown. Since this particular display is very busy and has a lot going on in a small area, there is no caption. The organization of this type of display is simple—in the sense that it is geometric and well balanced—but all of the components must be carefully measured and carefully placed. Therefore, this would probably be the type of display in which the students would collect the materials and the teacher would oversee and take a hand in the final layout. The result, as in figure 10, should be a display which reflects positively on both students and teacher.

V

DESIGN ELEMENTS AND PRINCIPLES

color, line, shape, texture, and space, and principles
of use—simplicity, emphasis, unity, and balance

The time has come to get down to the basics of display
technique—design elements and principles. There is nothing to
be leery of since most people have been using these basics for
years even though they may not have been aware of it. Each
time a person straightens a picture, tidies up his desk, or
moves a pillow or chair to a different location he is applying
some kind of order (design principle) and the object which was
moved or rearranged is a design element. In display work a
bulletin board is a shape and notices or whatever one puts on it
are design elements. A completed board, good or bad, is a design. Various shortcuts to good design are discussed in the next
chapter; here we begin with the basic elements: color, line,
shape, texture, and space.

Color

Since color is an important and indispensable tool for
anyone preparing displays, the various qualities and uses of
color must be mentioned. Many of the potentials of color may

be left unexploited, but one should know about them for they will affect art work whether or not they are used consciously. Therefore, we will briefly review some of the technical and psychological aspects of color before discussing their practical applications.

For practical purposes it is probably easiest to define color as a hue as distinct from black, white, and gray. Two of the commonly recognized properties or qualities of color are *value*, which refers to the relative lightness or darkness of a color, and *chroma*, or *intensity*, which refers to the relative strength or weakness of a color. Value is further subdivided into *tints*, or *pastels*, which applies to colors to which white has been added; and *shades*, which means colors to which black has been added. These terms may seem somewhat confusing at first, but the discussion should clarify their meaning.

There are three primary colors: yellow, blue, and red. These colors are mixed in various proportions to produce all the other colors (this concept relates only to "flat" colors and not to light rays, to which an entirely different color theory applies). When mixed in equal proportions these primary colors produce the secondary colors: yellow and blue make green, blue and red make purple, and red and yellow make orange. The six intermediate colors are produced with one primary color (which is named first) dominating in the mixture; they are yellow-green, blue-green, blue-purple, red-purple, red-orange, and yellow-orange. These are the generic, operating names but we usually encounter the colors under various fashion pseudonyms. In display work the thing to remember is that all of these colors are mixed from the primary colors of yellow, blue, and red; and that if we add white to any of these colors we have *tints*; and that if we add black, we have *shades*.

The color wheel shows these colors in their correct "mixing" relationship, and the wheel is used to determine the various types of color harmony. The color harmony which will be of most use in display work is the one involving *complementary* colors; complementary colors are those which are placed

40

Color Wheel

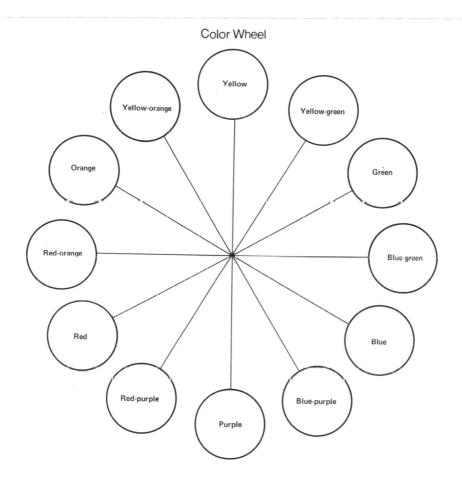

opposite each other on the color wheel. When placed side by side, complementary colors intensify each other; they are seldom used together in equal amounts since this divides attention, but a touch of orange used with blue will add snap to any display—and the same applies to red and green, yellow and purple, blue-purple and yellow-orange, and any other combinations of complementary colors. Another useful fact to know about complementary colors is that when they are mixed together in equal amounts, they produce neutral gray; therefore, if one is mixing colors and wishes to tone one down slightly without dulling it (as the addition of black would do), it can be done by means of the addition of a very small amount of the complementary color.

Another type of relationship is *monochromatic* harmony, which consists of tints and shades of one color. This harmony is too subtle for most display purposes, but it is often used in interior decoration. An *analogous* color harmony is made up of colors (usually three) which are side-by-side on the color wheel: blue-green, blue, and blue-purple would constitute an analogous harmony. Any of these three harmonies can be used alone or in combination; for instance, a monochromatic harmony based on blue can be enlivened by adding a touch of the complementary color, orange.

In addition to properties and harmonies, there are two other important aspects of color to be considered: colors can advance and recede (visually), and colors have certain psychological connotations. Red, red-orange, and yellow are often spoken of as "warm" colors, and blue, blue-green, and purple as "cool" colors. The warm colors seem to advance toward the observer and the cool colors to recede; intense colors also advance, and shades and tints recede. The applications of these factors to display work are rather obvious; seasonal displays should make use of colors appropriate to the temperature, and, in general, the intense, warm colors which seem to advance are more effective for posters than are the cool colors, and the tints and shades.

The warm and cool colors are, in part, the result of a psychological reaction (the warm colors suggest sun and fire, and cool colors suggest water and snow), but colors also have other inherent or acquired psychological meanings in addition to temperature. Green is restful; blue suggests melancholy; black is gloomy; white has connotations of purity, etc. Then there are groups of colors which have acquired certain connotations, such as red and green for stop and go, and red, white, and blue for patriotism. These associations of certain feelings with certain colors are rather generally accepted, but there are also individual reactions to color which often negate the supposed group response. Reliance on the psychological factors can be useful in display work, but, since individual response is often variable, one should not place too much faith in the psychological aspects of color.

Now we will cover somewhat the same ground in strictly practical terms: use intense colors and avoid the use of tints unless there is a definite reason for doing so. Limit displays to black and white (or tan) and one intense color, with a slight preference for warm colors which seem to advance. Order construction paper and poster board of good quality since the colors will usually have more intensity than those of cheaper materials. Try to avoid ordering assortments which have a high proportion of tints (most do); it would be better to order single packs of only a few intense colors and black and white than to be burdened with the tints. If ordering is done through a central service, try to make arrangements to acquire only what you need and want.

Use strong contrasts: light and dark, high and low intensity, and warm and cool colors. Stark white as a background is often too glaring, but off-white or tan is quite effective and materials such as natural burlap, grasscloth, or matchstick bamboo make excellent coverings for your boards. Though it may seem surprising (since black is supposed to have gloomy conotations), a matte (not glossy) black makes a highly effective background; light and intense colors spring to life against a black board. Furthermore, since most signs and display elements will be light in color, a black background will provide an automatic contrast.

Use dark accents on a light board and light accents on a dark one; use light, dark, light or dark, light, dark. This is not as vague as it may sound; it simply means that if the board is light and the display materials are also light (student reports for instance), something dark should be between the background and the display materials. If the background and display materials are both dark tones, then something light is needed to separate them—a sheet of white or yellow poster board or a piece of natural burlap.

In establishing strong contrasts, white, tan, and black are your chief allies. When planning a board or display it is best to think of it only in terms of light, dark, and one color. Another color may be added later, but if the initial planning includes only one color the result will usually be a simpler and more effective design. In most cases one color will be all that is needed, but a spot of the complementary color may be added for heightened effect. Remember at all times that good design is usually simple design; adding many colors will not disguise a poor design and it will usually add clutter rather than effect.

Line

Line is the second basic element in display work. For anyone doing displays, line has at least four different meanings and uses. For one thing, a line is a long mark which may be thick, thin, curved, or broken. This kind of line may be used to direct the eye or to wrap up an area as string does a package; in fact, use string, use rope, use wide strips of paper. Use a broken line; rectangles or squares of paper (dark if they are to be used on a light surface, and light if on dark) used in a row are much more effective than a solid line would be.

These lines can move across a surface to direct the eye where you wish it to go—to another part of the design, to a block of text, or to a display item or object. They can also wrap up groups of items in order to relate them to one another and separate them from the rest of the design. For example, black or white rug yarn can be used to "wrap up" a group of notices or book reports; this device will tie the various elements together in a design sense (they will become a square or rectangle of design rather than a group of miscellaneous materials) and will set them off and make them more important. As with colors, certain lines have certain psychological effects. Horizontal lines suggest solidity and repose; vertical lines suggest strength; diagonal lines are dynamic, and curved lines are suggestive of movement. Repetition of a line reinforces the feeling it suggests, and crossing lines create an area of high interest where two lines intersect.

A line is also the edge where two shapes meet; two sheets of paper placed side by side have a "line" between them; if one sheet is small and is placed on top of the other, there is a contour line around the edge of the smaller sheet. A line is a row of things: a row of circles, a row of papers, a row of notices. A row can function in much the same way as a drawn or painted line; it can lead the eye along and it elicits the same psychological reactions—a vertical arrangement will suggest strength, a diagonal arrangement will by dynamic, and so on. All of these lines have to be "aimed"; they should not be scattered about at random and shoot off in diverse directions. You have to decide what part of the design is most important and then reinforce it and direct attention to it by judicious use of lines. Since you have a variety of different ones from which to choose, select the ones most appropriate to your purpose.

There is one other line which can play a large part in your design; it is an invisible line which might be called a margin line. A page of print has a definite margin at top, bottom, and sides, and if there are illustrations they are lined up in accord with this margin; this edge line is a very important part of the page layout. Since this margin is not drawn in—except by your eye—it is an invisible line. A bulletin board, poster, or display has the same kind of invisible line involved in the layout, and an effort should be made to have a margin on at least two sides of the design. Usually a four-sided margin would be impossible because of the diverse size and shape of the display materials; but the bottom row of items could be aligned along the lower edge, and the items could be aligned at the right.

There should also be some margin lines within the design: the bottom of a cartoon could be in line with the top or bottom of a block of print or a row of display items; a caption could be in line at the top with the top of a cartoon and the left side could be in line with other items displayed; any kind of row should be in line with something else in the design. The more items to be displayed the more need there is for these invisible lines, for without them the design will look like a hodge podge. Attention to line does not mean that all the elements in a design must be lined up—they need not be—but some things must be. The board should be designed with this principle kept in mind, or a tentative arrangement of materials should be made and the elements moved around as required in order to achieve the essential margins.

Shape

The third element is shape. A shape is a form—round, square, big, little, regular, or irregular. The bulletin board itself has a shape, usually a rectangle. Everything which is put on it is a shape; the design elements chosen may be of any shape but the printed items are almost always rectangles. The chief problem is to arrange all of the different size and different shape items into larger and more important shapes and then to relate them to the rest of the design.

The first thing to remember about background shapes is to keep them large and simple. Stick to basic shapes such as squares, rectangles, circles, and triangles for background. For special emphasis use variations on punctuation-mark shapes such as an asterisk, question mark, or exclamation point; these are cleancut shapes with built-in meaning and emphasis—they are also good design. Avoid free forms such as amorphous, cloudlike shapes; they are usually just fillers and detract from

46

the design. Make large and bold shapes with simple contour lines; use as few shapes as possible and do not use two or three shapes where one large one could be used.

The second thing to remember about shapes is not to mix them too much: rectangles and squares are usually unavoidable; therefore, if possible, use only one other shape. Use one large triangle or three adjoining or overlapping triangles (odd numbers are more interesting than even, so when repeating a shape, do so twice rather than once); use one or three large circles as a background and then smaller circles as emphasis within the design. Try to limit the different sizes used; as a general rule, use only two sizes of the same shape, and make the difference in size extreme.

Texture

Element number four is texture. Texture is the visual or tactile appearance of a surface. Surfaces can look or feel smooth, rough, soft, hard, cool, or warm; they can look pleasant or unpleasant to touch. Certain combinations of texture have special appeal: smooth and rough, cool and warm, natural and man-made. You mix textures in your home; a nubby material on a couch against a smooth wall, a furry rug on a polished floor, wood grain against a brick wall, and fragile curtains against rough textured drapes. Your house would be dull if there were no contrast in surface texture; the same applies to a display or bulletin board.

Use smooth poster board against natural burlap; make use of rough textured paper or vinyl backgrounds; use fabric, corrugated cardboard (but beware of insipid tints), grasscloth beach mats, textured place mats (especially good for displaying photographs), and yarn and rope for line. Natural fabrics and textures are especially good for backgrounds because they have a high recognition factor (we know how they feel) and provide texture contrast with any paper object displayed against them. Since most printed material has no tactile quality, texture is an especially valuable and striking ingredient for made-to-order displays.

Space

The fifth and last element is space. Space is depth, the third dimension, objects that are in front of or behind other things —or around them or projecting from them. Space adds interest, excitement, and contrast to your design. It is also easy to add. Plan the board "flat" and then look at it in terms of space; how would it look if that circle, square, or caption projected a bit? Project it. A small item can be projected by attaching it to a small cardboard box and then attaching the box to the display, and there are also easy methods of folding cardboard or poster board which will give a 3-D effect. Even more simple, any shape that overlaps another seems to be in front of it; and warm colors, as we have already mentioned, seem to be in front of cool ones. If one is using a cartoon figure, it is easy to make an arm and hand project from the board; if the hand is holding something, so much the better. An object can be displayed easily by constructing a shelf and attaching it to the board. Anything which adds depth or the appearance of depth will add to the effectiveness of any display.

There you have it; those are all of the elements of design: color, line, shape, texture, and space. We now go on to a few of the mix and match rules for using them. These rules are simplicity, emphasis, unity, and balance.

Simplicity

Simplicity is clearness and lack of complication. It is the use of only a few colors or black and white and one color; it is the use of only one or two basic shapes and only one or two different sizes of these shapes; it is simple organization of your materials. It is clearness and economy in selection of the idea or ideas to be sold; if an attempt is made to sell too much at one time, nothing will be sold. Stick to one or two ideas or products at a time; tell a minimum about them; be economical in the selection of color as well as of shape and texture; and organize the materials as simply as possible.

48

Emphasis

Emphasis is the stress or prominence given to an idea or design element. It is making one idea, color, shape, or texture dominant and others subordinate—if all of these elements are of equal interest, no one of them will receive attention. Emphasize only the dominant idea or shape by making it larger, brighter, more textured; surround it with empty space, lead into it with lines, point to it with a fat arrow, make it project from the board. Every design has to have one main center of interest if it is to make a point; there may be secondary items and areas of interest but these should not compete with the central idea. A center of interest in terms of idea must be chosen, and then design elements must be utilized to make it the center of design interest.

Unity

One definition of unity is "singleness of effect or style"; another is "totality of related parts." In display work unity is often a simple matter of repetition and consistency. It is the overlapping of three identical shapes in different colors. It is use of a large square and a few smaller ones elsewhere in the design. It is use of any shape, color, line, or texture with a repeat of it elsewhere in the design. It is the repetition of similar elements in a different size or color. It is consistency in the style of lettering. Each of the elements in any design should mesh with every other element and should relate to the whole so that a single effect is achieved.

Balance

The dictionary defines balance as a "weight, force, or influence countering the effect of another." This is acceptable as a starting point, but the real problem is in determining the visual weight of various design elements; some textures and colors weigh more than others in a design sense, and this visual weight varies depending on the environment. Balance in a design is achieved when the visual weight of the elements on one side of a display is equal to the visual weight of the elements on the other side. The elements can be divided equally to create formal balance, or a trickier and more effective informal balance can be attempted (informal balance is based more on arrangement than on actual weight). Formal balance is much easier to determine and handle and so it is particularly recommended when there are many items to be displayed. When working with a single idea or item, informal balance is often the better solution. Balance is something which really has to be seen, and the illustrations in this book point out various kinds and applications of balance.

VI

DESIGN COMPONENTS

basic background shapes, multipurpose cartoons,

and cutouts

The shortcut techniques to good design referred to earlier are not intended to eliminate planning publicity in advance, nor are they a substitute for creative designing of bulletin boards and displays. They are simplified design techniques to assist in planning displays and to help in achieving maximum results with minimum time and effort. The fact that many of these techniques are simple, adaptable, and reasonably foolproof is due to their being based on design principles and effective advance planning.

Illustrations 11 through 16 preview a few of the techniques which will be discussed and explained in this chapter. Figures 11 and 12 are displays based on the use of negative and positive shapes. The display in figure 11 is black and white except for red lettering and a red burlap background; the face in figure 12 employs an even more limited color range, black and white against a tan background. However in spite of this limited color range (or because of it), the geometric shapes and strong contrast create an effective display. Figures 13 and 14

51

are cutout display components of a bus and a house; a few line and cutout extras have been added, but, here too, the basic shapes are geometric. The owl in figure 15 is another very simple shape, and the bug in figure 16 may look complicated but is made from a grouping of basic shapes. Each of these display set-ups or components is easily executed, requires little or no art skill, lends itself to a variety of display uses, and is adaptable and reusable. Now to explain how these components and techniques, and others, are designed and combined.

The first two techniques, which are separate but related, are the use of simple, geometric shapes and the use of positive and negative space. The latter technique undoubtedly requires some explanation and that, perhaps, can best be done by describing the process. Suppose that a circle is cut from the middle of a piece of poster board; the circle should be centered and if the board is the usual 22 by 28 inch size, the diameter of the circle should be about 16 or 17 inches. The circle must be cut in such a way that the background is left in one piece (if a "cut-in" is made the edges can be taped together from the back). The cutout circle is a positive shape and the hole left in the piece of poster board is a negative shape. Placed side by side, the positive and negative shapes produce an instant design background which is both simple and effective.

This positive-negative technique can be used with any shape but is most effective with common geometric shapes and with large arrows and asterisks. If some of the same shapes are cut in different sizes and colors, both positive and negative shapes can be used in different combinations; to add variety, some of the forms could be covered with burlap or other printed or textured fabrics. At least a few of the shapes should be cut in the largest possible size that can be used on school bulletin boards. Poster board and construction paper can be purchased in large sizes, and it might be possible to have some of the shapes cut from 4 by 8 foot sheets of fiberboard. One might start with only a few shapes but these should be added to as time and the budget permit; the more there are on hand, the easier it should be to design displays.

11

12

13

14

15

16

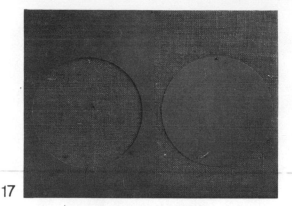

17

Examples of a few shapes and ways in which they can be used might help to clarify the potential usefulness of these techniques. Figure 17 shows a piece of poster board which has been cut to cover half the bulletin board space; a large circle has been cut out and the wide top margin makes allowance for a caption. The "positive" circle is placed opposite the "negative" circle and the background design is finished (of course the textured background material helps the design considerably). Figures 18 through 20 show ways in which this background design might be used for different types of displays.

Figure 18 is a quiz with a large caption, a brief text done in "marking pen cursive," and the quiz answer under a lift panel (A lift panel is a piece of poster board which is hinged at the top with tape, either on the front or underneath, and which has a tape lift tab at the bottom). This quiz lends itself to a display series about the school, student activities, or faculty, and only new questions and answers are needed for each change. The lift panel is, of course, a gimmick and the display may be done without it; the question or questions may be written on a block

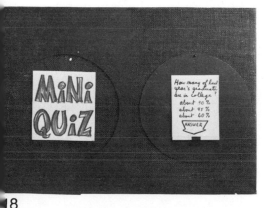

18

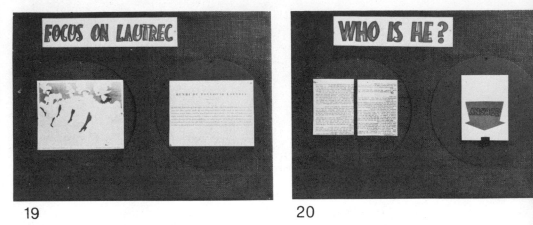

19   20

of poster board and the answer written in very small print at the bottom.

Illustration 19 employs a caption, art reproduction, and a brief biography. This approach is similar to the "Spotlight on Thoreau" display in figure 11, though that display combines a sketch of an author with biographical and critical information. Both displays may be developed as a series dealing with artists' and authors' lives and works, and one might use printed, photocopied, or student prepared materials. Figure 20 adds a twist by presenting the biography or critical evaluation in the form of a quiz—with the answer under another lift panel. A somewhat different arrangement would be to post the answer nearby, eliminate the lift panel, and add a drawing or photo of the subject.

For a quick and space filling seasonal display, the negative space might contain a large caption proclaiming "Spring" and the positive circle can frame a large, colorful, cutout flower. A large snowflake might be used for a winter bulletin board, a leaf for fall, and a large, stylized sun for summer. Holidays can be represented in the same fashion— a large caption in one space and one basic, "representative" shape in the other. Most symbolic shapes, especially those associated with holidays, have become trite from overuse; when they are used they should be large and starkly simple in outline. The bulletin boards shown and discussed have all used a two circle back-

54

ground, but, if the bulletin board is large, or the display materials small, a four or six circle background might be preferable.

Elliptical positive and negative shapes are shown in figure 21, and figures 22 and 23 offer design variations and uses. Two white circles suggest the pupils of an eye, and they may be moved from side to side or up and down depending on where attention is to be directed. The display might tell one to "Look At," "See," or "Watch" something—the something may be an adjoining bulletin board or easel display, a classroom exhibit or activity, or a special announcement. If a profile face is used, the announcement can be printed in a quotation "balloon" as is done in figure 23. The smiling face of figure 12 could welcome students, parents, or special visitors to the school for special events, or could report on successful school activities; a frown could be used when the team loses or the school picnic is postponed. If a bulletin board is very large, the face may be designed to fit half the space with related display materials occupying the other half.

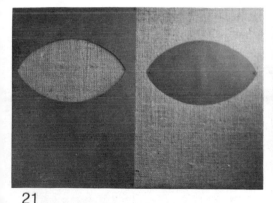

21

22

23

The circle and ellipitical backgrounds shown were designed with the negative block covering half the bulletin board space. This technique may also be used with a rectangular cutout (or cutouts) and many of the same types of display materials may be used. A rectangular background, however, permits the display of more materials than designs using a circle or ellipse; this can be either an advantage or disadvantage depending on the number and size of items to be used. In any case, rectangular cutouts should be carefully planned for maximum usefulness to you; you might wish to plan for display of 8½ by 11 inch pages of student work, or you might size the background to accommodate a series of large reproductions or study prints. Measure your cutouts accordingly.

Rectangular positive and negative shapes are shown in figure 24. In this example the larger shape is less than half the size of the bulletin board permitting greater variety in arrangement. The smaller rectangle is cut so that its long side is equal to the short side of the larger shape; this was done so that the shapes will "match" when placed as they are in figure 24. The negative shape was also cut to accommodate four papers when placed vertically (see figure 25) and three when placed horizontally (see figures 26 and 27). This requires some trial and error in measuring, but since the shapes will be used over and over again, the effort involved is well worth it. Figures 24 through 27 suggest only a few of the possible arrangements and uses of these highly versatile positive-negative shapes.

The positive and negative backgrounds we have been discussing are designs which produce fast and effective results and which require minimum maintenance; for these reasons they are particularly useful for hallway boards which tend to become neglected areas. They can be equally useful in a classroom, but, since they provide little space for learning materials (especially the circle and ellipse), their classroom use must be carefully considered—they should not become merely decorative space fillers.

One educational possibility, which has already been in-

24   25

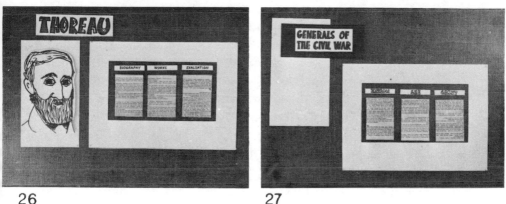

26   27

dicated, is to use the space for a display series—using study prints, fact sheets, reproductions, math problems, map symbols, historic documents, or any of the series of educational materials available in standard sizes. One might have students do assignments on famous people, cities, states, countries, inventions, science experiments, book reviews, poetry, short stories, or essays. Standard size requirements should be made for student work; this makes the display easier to maintain, and, because the material must fit on a certain size page or card, it offers students practice in "made to measure" writing. A culminating display might combine the whole series of professional, teacher-, or student-prepared materials into one large exhibit.

57

Rectangles are less interesting than other shapes, but, as we saw with negative-positive shapes, they are useful design backgrounds. They are particularly effective backgrounds when the items to be displayed are either numerous or of differing sizes; the psychologically stable shape of a rectangle seems to help pull multiple or diverse objects into a unified whole. Figure 28 shows three red rectangles (the top one to be used for a caption) and figure 29 has added more interest by halving one of the large shapes. Figure 29 also shows how this background helps pull smaller shapes (notices or student work) into design units.

Figure 30 shows an even simpler arrangement using only two blue rectangles. In figure 31 smaller shapes have been placed against a background; note that the shapes "stick out" but that the large rectangle still holds them together in a design unit. In figure 32 the same background shapes are used to pull diverse size items into a unit. Figure 33 shows a large display which uses six shapes as a background for varied material.

The advantages of these display backgrounds are multiple. The backgrounds are easy to prepare; they require no art talent whatsoever; they are effective; they are adaptable; and they require minimum care and feeding. Any time a rush display is needed, one need only select a few basic ingredients (background shapes) and add a dash of spice (caption, comment, quotation, reproduction, study print, map). Bulletin boards can be kept fresh by retaining the background shapes and changing the "spice" often. When it is time for a complete change of scene, a new set of basic ingredients can be selected and the old ones stored for future use.

Preparation of cartoon and caption assortments is another technique reducing the time needed to assemble individual displays. The main requirement of this technique is creative, long-range planning. It must be decided which cartoons and captions are most useful and how they can be combined most effectively. If the cartoons are to be used for hallway displays, some of them should cover from one fourth to one third of the

58

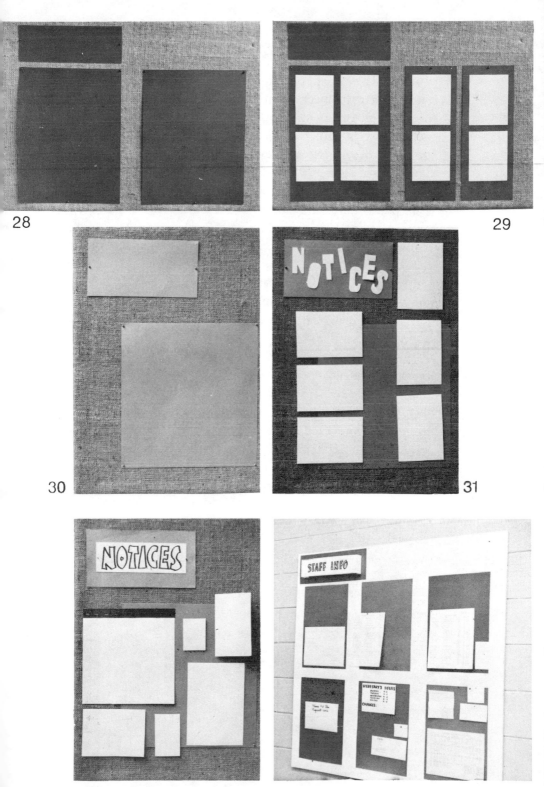

28

29

30

31

32

33

background space and the captions should be a proportionate size. Cartoons and captions for classroom use should be smaller to leave more space for display materials. But size is a relative thing; the designer must decide the size of the display components that will offer the greatest design flexibility in each individual situation. Some of the cartoons which will be suggested are simple enough to be copied by almost anyone; others might require the skills of an art student.

Figure 34 is a man with his head full of dates. He may be used in a display quiz matching these dates with events of the Revolutionary War (if the events are on separate blocks of poster board they may be used later for other displays). The display may be handled in step-by-step fashion with each event added to the display as it is discussed in class. Another possibility is to direct attention to only one date at a time. An asterisk can be placed by Dec. 1773 and the board can display materials or student reports related to events of that month; in a few days the asterisk can be moved to the next date and the material changed.

Old 34 can be used for other types of displays by giving his brain a new poster board cover; one might use colored poster board or different colors for each section of his brain. His head can be full of dates; people; events; cities, states, or countries; mathematics problems; experiments; famous paintings; literary works; types of reference books; kinds of reading; school activities and events; occupations; or what have you.

34

35

Figure 35 is selling "Hot Off The Presses," "Latest News From The Civil War," "Special Edition on the Space Flight," or any kind of hot news—current or historical—which you wish him to promote. If the news is foreign or historical the paper boy might be given different clothes, or perhaps just a different hat. He would be useful for a hallway display dealing with school activities, and if there were relatively few notices he could be made very large as a space filler. In the classroom he might be introducing a new unit of study. A display of this type might feature a newspaper style article on the unit ("Miss Brown announced today that a new unit was in preparation ...."); other articles could feature student response to the announcement and highlights of the unit.

This type of display might be turned over to students, and they could select rotating editorial writers, columnists, and political cartoonists. It might be directed to current events (either classroom, school, local or nationwide), and it might have special issues concerning special people, "weeks," events, or places, units of study, hobbies, or anything else appropriate for the class. All of these display materials should, however, be arranged in some way—a caption and cartoon alone do not make an organized display. Blocks of poster board might be alloted for different articles, and sections of the newspaper could be given subheadings.

Figure 36 has something to show or tell about. His coat lining could give information on school events and activities, special awards, scholarships, new courses, changes in class or school hours, new books in the library, or new faculty

36

37   38

members. Possible captions are "Pssst," "Latest Info," "Hot Tips on the Team," "Check This," or "For Insiders Only." Since most of the notices will be light in color the coat lining would provide more contrast if it were a dark color, and it would be more interesting if a dark fabric were used. In the classroom the coat man could offer news about individual students, class activities, test results, or units of study.

Figure 37 looks as though he might just have had a bright idea or remembered something; a lightbulb (real or cutout) might be placed above his head to emphasize it. His idea could be about a program, exhibit, or varsity game he wishes to attend, a field trip for which he must remember the fare, a type of reading material he needs, a reference source to use for a term paper, or a change of schedule he had almost forgotten. He might be saying "I Mustn't Forget," "I Almost Forgot," "That's What I Need," or "That's Where I Should Look." Or he might be reminded "Don't Forget," "Remember the Date," "Check Dictionary Supplements," or "Have You Thought of . . . ?"

Figure 38 is "blowing his horn" about something of great importance. His caption might read "Hear Ye, Hear Ye," "Attention All," "Heed This," "Gather 'Round," "We Are

Proud to Announce," or "Presenting." In the classroom his announcement would be related to class events or students; as a general display he can be directing attention to almost anything. His horn can be make long enough to extend the width of the board and an appropriate banner hung from it. Another possibility is to have the announcement coming out of the horn in a balloon of print.

Figure 39 has something he wishes to show off and he seems very pleased about the whole thing. He might be "Presenting," "Announcing," or "Introducing" whatever it is he has to show. Figure 40 also has something he wants to tell about but he is being rather shy or modest about his news. He might be saying "We Don't Wish to Boast, BUT," "We're Rather Proud," or "We're Awfully Pleased." Either of these two figures can direct attention to winning sport scores, school scores on competitive tests, or to any type of personal, group, or school achievement; in the classroom they can refer to test or project results, or to any relevant class activity. Though the figures can introduce the same type of material, the captions will differ to fit the demean of each character.

Figure 41 is a twin brother of figure 40 but he is upset rather than pleased about his news. "We Blew It," "We'll Do Better

42

Next Time," "I'm Sorry to Tell You," "I Hate to Say It," "We're Most Upset," or "We're Very Sorry" are all captions which match his doleful expression. He can present results of not-so-successful endeavors, unexpected delays of one kind or another, or can make a tongue-in-cheek introduction of a unit of study ("I hate to tell you ... but we're going to study fractions").

The ready-for-the-hunt figure 42 can be captioned "Look No Further," "Looking for Something? Try (a particular type of reference source)," "It's Big Game Time" (for sports events), "Take Aim" (on a college or career), or "Get on the Mark" (with a type of reading). Far from being a fearless hunter, figure 43 is obviously scared; he might need captions telling him "Don't Be Shy," "It Doesn't Bite," "It Won't Hurt to Try," or "Aw Come On and Use It." He might be used to introduce information on the library or reference

43

44

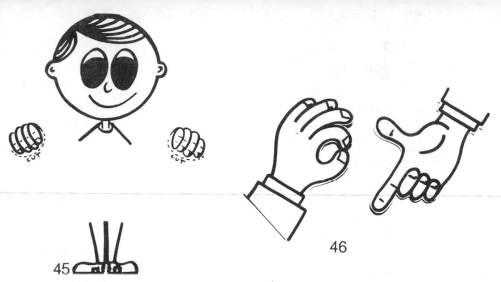

45

46

sources, on mathematics principles, spelling rules, science experiments, creative writing, or some group activity.

A special dish is being served by figure 44 and captions for him might be "Especially For You," "*Pièce de Résistance*," "Blue Plate Special," "Best in the House," or "Our Own Concoction." He might be "serving" student work, special activities, a new course, new equipment, new school policy, or anything of special interest.

Figure 45 can be used to accommodate almost any kind of notice. He can be made a large size and used on a bulletin board, or he can be propped up and used as a 12-inch stand atop a table. Since he will probably be holding a light colored notice, he should either be cut out and mounted on dark colored poster board or shown holding a dark piece of board to which light colored notices may be attached. He will add attractiveness to any kind of notice, even a hastily scribbled one. If the hands of the figure are cut out entirely, they may be moved around on the display board and used to hold almost anything from the top, bottom or sides. In addition to notices, the figure might be holding an example of student work, a study print, a map, a magazine, a pamphlet, or a small object.

Figure 46 shows two kinds of hands which can have multiple uses in display work. The "holding" hand can be used almost anywhere to call attention to directions or happenings. If the cartoon hand is drawn life size, it can be mounted on poster board and propped on desks and shelves, or attached to book-cases, cabinets, windows, or walls. If the thumb on the cartoon hand is left unglued, notices may easily be slipped underneath it. The pointing hand can direct attention to almost anything, and it will be particularly useful in directing visitors to a meeting or open house (a number of hands might be run off on a copy machine and used to make a path to the right place).

These are only a few suggestions for mix-and-match components, but the cartoons and captions mentioned form a basic kind of repertory company. One need only assemble the members and assign roles and captions. Other cartoons and captions should, of course, be added, and each addition will increase the flexibility and effectiveness of any display program.

Now all that the repertory company needs are a few props—large poster board cutouts. Most cutouts should be as large as possible and simple in outline; details, texture, and dimension may be added later but the basic form must be simple and clean cut. Figure 47 shows a basic cutout of a bus and figure 13 shows the same bus with a few additions. One might add wheels from a child's toy or construction set, aluminum foil chrome strips, acetate windows, or cartoon faces in the windows. Possible captions are "We're All Going," "Get on Board," "Take a Trip" (through the U.S., through history, a foreign country, literature, fairy tales, the countryside, or the city). The display used with the cutout could utilize pictures, study prints, student work, or books. Another possibility is to design a display to be used before and

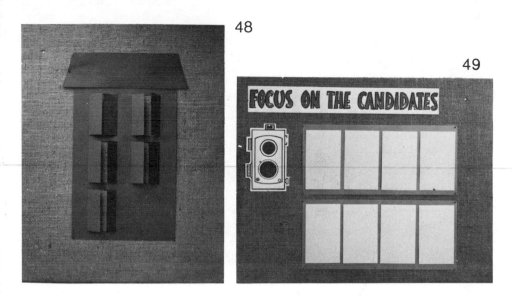

after a field trip to point out what to look for and then to comment on what was seen.

A house cutout is pictured in figure 48, and figure 14 shows how it might look after some design rehabilitation. Windows and window sills have been added, "I" shaped cuts in the windows have been opened out to make shutters, and a backing sheet of white paper provides window panes for the shuttered windows. Note that the window panes were drawn in freehand; the slight irregularity of the panes (and of the door panels and shutter lines) adds a touch of individuality to the design—but the lines should not be too irregular and detract from the design.

In lower grades small photos of the students or their names could be placed in the windows with a "We Live Here" caption; if the house cutout is very large it can be used to display student work on a rotating basis ("Best in the House"). An added use is to show the letters, words, numbers, colors, books, or objects the class is studying. An anticipation factor is added since the shutters can cover the items until the teacher or a student shows them.

A camera cutout is part of the display shown in figure 49, and this type of cutout can be used to "Focus On" almost anything. This particular display is set up to display student work and a possible arrangement of materials is illustrated; two large background rectangles are used to pull the individual items into units. One large background shape would also be effective and the elements might be "tied" together in a rectangle of rug yarn. The cutout might be on a tripod or held by a cartoon figure. A similar idea is a transistor radio for "Tune In" or "We're Tuned In" captions.

Birds and animals are good cutout possibilities, but they are somewhat more complicated than buses and houses. Cartoons of living things usually must be copied or adapted from some source or another, and one of the problems involves selecting the "right" source. Among the idea sources are display books and pamphlets; cartoon advertisements; children's books (an excellent source is *Ed Emberley's Drawing Book of Animals*†); and catalogs for children's books, filmstrips, and other visual aids. Cartoon art is getting better and better but unfortunately there are many illustrations (especially those done for children) which are trite and poorly executed; one selection criterion is to avoid illustrations which look like comic or coloring book art.

Look at the two birds in figure 50. The top cutout might be

†Little Brown & Co., Boston, 1970.

acceptable for a bulletin board (barely), but the bottom cutout has much more style and character. The bottom bird is just as easy to draw and cut out as the other, and it is sophisticated enough to appeal to all age groups—not just to children. The bottom bird will have even more appeal to teenagers and adults if it is a non-bird color and perhaps even plaid, striped, or spotted. Possible captions include all the birdy ones such as "Birds of a Feather" (flock to the school play), "The Early Bird" (gets tickets to the game), "Not Just for the Birds," and "We're Flying High." If props are added (nest, birdhouse, cage, limb, articles of clothing, and even a book, cutout suitcase or satchel, or sign), the caption possibilities increase to "Feather Your Nest," "Don't be a Stay-at-Home," "Go Out on a Limb," "Dress for Spring," "It's Travel Time," "We've a Satchel of Career Ideas," and so forth.

Figure 15, the wise owl cutout, can be used with usual owl sayings and he too can be given props. He can wear a mortar board and glasses, carry an umbrella, or hold a book under his wing. He can offer advice on a variety of subjects and he can also be "Out on a Limb" as he is in figure 15. The bug in figure 16 is a bit complicated but all his component parts are simple shapes. He can be a book, hobby, travel, history, neatness, or reference source "bug;" he can put a "Bug in Your Ear," or be a "We Don't Want to Bug You" bug.

We have already discussed use of geometric shapes as backgrounds, but these shapes are equally useful as design motifs; the shapes are easy to cut, versatile, and suggest ideas for displays. Figures 51 through 54 indicate some of the possibilities. The "Get in the Swim" caption might be used for any type of activity. Figure 52 might be captioned "Follow the Crowd"

51   52

53   54

and could encourage attendance at some function. In figure 53 the minnows of figure 52 become petals, and larger ellipse shapes are leaves. The design might be used with a spring or summer display, a "Pick a Reference Source" display (petals could be numbered to correspond with listed reference sources), or a "We're Growing Too" display directing attention to school growth and achievement. Figure 54 can be used with school announcements, or the record idea can be applied to "Report Hit Parade," "Take a Spin with These Books," "Get in the Right Groove," or "LP Career Ideas."

Some other possible combinations are:

1. A bulletin board could be covered with large black squares in a checkerboard pattern, with cutouts of checker or chess pieces, and captions such as "It's Your Move," "Plan Your Strategy," "Don't Get Cornered," and "Learn Winning Ways." The display could deal with career planning, research methods, consumer education, etiquette and grooming, or health.

2. A cartoon man could be carried "Up, Up, and Away" by three large circle balloons. Captions include "LSD Isn't the Only Way to Travel," "Is This Flight Necessary?" and "Take off with Books."

3. A cartoon figure shown "Behind the 8 Ball" could be

offered activities to take his mind off his problems or help him to solve them.

4. A cartoon figure could be "Boxed in" by three large squares and he too could be offered advice on how to solve his dilemma.

5. A large circle plate with cutout silverware might be "serving" a selection of student work, a choice of activities, or an assortment of books. The display could also be offering new courses or advertising a student banquet.

Naturally all of these props should be carefully dismantled and stored along with the backgrounds, characters, and captions. All items from the publicity repertory should be stage ready at any time so repairing, refurbishing, and replacing should be constant. Since most display ideas are old, the ingredients should be new, at least in appearance.

And it must be admitted that none of the display ideas in this chapter is entirely new; most are adaptations or new combinations of rather standard ingredients—but that, for the most part, is what display work is all about. Any or all of the ideas may be imitated (but not reproduced) to help get you started or adapted to keep you going. It is best to remember that there are few, if any, entirely new ideas, and that it is impossible to make each display new and different. However, it is possible to make each display fresh and imaginative and that should be the goal of anyone doing displays.

VII

LETTERING, LAYOUT, AND CARTOONING

basic skills, short-cuts and tricks for
the untrained

Lettering

Many people regard lettering as one of the most difficult and frustrating aspects of display work. Much of this frustration is due to the commonly held belief that plain, simple letters should be the easiest to execute, and that failing to do these adequately, there is absolutely no point in attempting other kinds of letters. It is true that lettering, even among commercial artists, is a speciality requiring long hours of study and practice. But it is also true that the thin, straight, and seemingly simple lettering attempted by most amateurs is actually the most difficult to do freehand, without a ruler or some other mechanical aid. No attempt will be made to teach this kind of "simple" lettering. If one should have a facility for lettering, it is worth while to develop it; but if one is rather inept, and most of us are in that category, it is more expedient to learn only a few, adaptable types of freehand lettering and to rely on lettering kits and prepared letters for variety.

The easiest, fastest, and most adaptable lettering for an

73

amateur is a type which involves combining two rather sloppy kinds of letters: a simple painted letter, and an outline letter executed with a felt marking pen. The technique is very simple and the materials required are:

- a flat brush at least ¼-inch in width;
- a black, felt marking pen with a wide tip;
- poster paint, preferably red, blue, or green;
- a number of 2-inch or 3-inch strips of white poster board.

The brush should be loaded with paint, and, using the flat of the brush, a word or phrase should be printed on a strip of poster board (paper should not be used since it tends to curl when paint is applied). The letters should be fat and "juicy." They may be sloppy and uneven but that is not important; it is important, however, to keep the letters simple with no extra curlicues or curves. The top line of figure 55 shows how this type of letter might look; if lettering is shaggier than the example that is unimportant. Since the paint has to dry thoroughly before the second step, it might be best to paint a number of practice strips at one time. When lettering is being done for a sign or poster, it is best to pencil in the text and margin lines, but this is not necessary for a practice session.

Step two, when the painted letters have dried, is to outline the letters with a marking pen. The full width of the tip should be used in order to make a fat outline, and the wide side of the marker may be used for an even wider line. No attempt should

be made to outline the letters exactly; outlining should be done quickly and loosely with some overlapping of the painted letters and some gaps. The middle line of figure 55 shows the kind of outline letter to be used, and the bottom line of figure 55 shows how the two types of letters look in combination. What has been done is to combine two kinds of casual (or sloppy) letters to achieve an easy and effective kind of display letter.

This type of lettering might also be made with two felt markers, one colored marker for the base letter and another for outlining. A marking pen is easier to use than a brush, and since the ink dries instantly it is a faster method than painting. Some marking pens have washable inks but indelible colors are preferable because the color tends to be brighter and more permanent. Poster paint, however, is more intense in color than any felt markers and its use adds interesting texture, especially if the paint is somewhat thick. An added benefit is that different size brushes permit greater flexibility in letter size. A painted basic letter is usually worth the extra effort involved, but it is a matter of personal choice.

Different effects may be achieved by varying the materials and techniques. Painting may be done with a dry brush and rather dry paint for a "brushy" stroke, or thick globby paint may be used. A black marking pen is the usual choice for outlining, but other colors may be preferred; one could combine blue paint and a blue marker, blue and red markers, or any desired colors. Outline letters can be effective used alone, but executing them is not as simple as it might seem; at first one tends to get "lost" and lose the shape of the letter. After outlining solid letters for a time though, it becomes much easier to make outline letters separately.

All of the letters discussed can be made as large or small as one wishes. Small painted letters can be executed with a small, pointed brush (sable brushes are more expensive but they last longer, hold a point better, and shed hairs less than the cheaper bristle brushes), and a fine tipped fiber pen may be used for outlining. Larger letters require using the broad side of a wide, flat brush and outlining with the broad side of a felt marker. Marking pens come in various sizes, and extra strokes can be used for larger base or outline letters. Letters may be expanded or compressed to meet individual needs; examples are shown in figure 56.

Cutout letters are very useful for display purposes. Here too, amateurs often attempt to make the thin, straight letters which are the most difficult to do. The thinner the cutout letters the more difficult it is to keep them straight and of even thickness, and the harder it is to handle them. The letters at the top of figure 57 have been carefully cut but there are still variations in thickness and regularity. If cutout letters are as fat and blocky as possible (as in the middle of figure 57), they are easier to cut and to handle, and they are more effective for displays. All letters except the "I" can be cut from the same size square or rectangle, and the absolute minimum should be cut away. The "holes" may be skipped entirely or they may be punched out later with a small ring punch, and, in this case, only one ring hole should be punched in a letter regardless of the letter size. This is one of the few cases where, due to convenience of cutting, it is better to use construction paper rather than poster board.

Dark letters should be used on light board and light letters should be used on a dark board. One very simple and attractive trick is to switch the dark-light arrangement in the middle of a word or phrase. If, for example, one half of a display is blue and the other half is white, the lettering can be designed to cross from the white to the blue background. Blue letters would be used against the white and white letters would be used against the blue (see the bottom line of figure 57).

A very useful technique is to make or place the letters on strips of poster board. One must estimate the space to be filled, the amount of text, and then cut strips of poster board (preferably of the same size) to fit the situation. Lettering on strips makes it much easier to keep letters and margins even; there is little chance of down-hill slope; mistakes can be discarded easily; strips are easy to save and reuse; and the

76

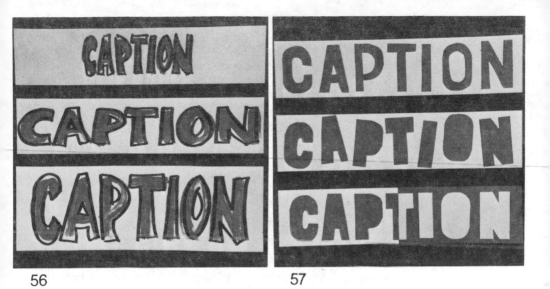

56   57

strips are an excellent design device. If one has several "blocks" of text (information about places, events, or people) these can be done on "blocks" of poster board. The blocks will be easy to arrange on the displays and easy to store and reuse later, either together or in different combinations.

Figures 58 and 59 demonstrate some of the steps and problems involved in lettering captions on strips. Figure 58 shows two beginning strips for a caption; the top caption was executed with poster paint and the lower with a marking pen. In both examples, top and bottom margins were penciled in to keep the lettering in a straight line. If the caption strip must be a particular length, the letters should also be lettered in to be sure they will fit the available space; if size requirements are flexible the lettering can be done on a long strip which can be cut off at the end of the lettering. A comparison of the two examples will show that the painted letters are more uneven (a brush is harder to control) but, as has been mentioned, they are more intense in color than the inked letters. Marking-pen letters used for captions usually require extra strokes for greater visibility; the letters at the beginning of the lower caption in figure 58 are extra stroke letters while those at the end of the word "candidate" are single stroke letters.

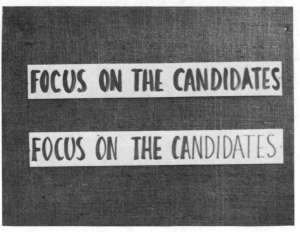

58

The first two lines of figure 59 show both captions as they look when outlined; the wide outlining even improves the too thin letters in the word candidate. The bottom line of this figure shows thin marking-pen letters outlined with thin letters—the result is less than satisfactory. The key to using these outline letters effectively is to keep them fat and loose. In all the examples shown the outlining is gappy and overlapping, and, for those who have tried "careful" lettering, some unlearning may be necessary before getting the feel of this type of lettering.

There are many advantages in being able to do one's own lettering: after a bit of practice, hand lettering (with the exception of cutout letters) is usually faster than most other

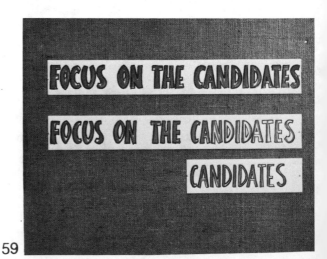

59

methods; one is able to choose the exact size and color desired; lettering kits are often short of needed letters and letters are often broken, bent, or discolored; and "handmade" letters can be much more attractive and effective than commercial letters. There are, of course, many times when lettering kits can be of use. Mitten letters (plaster letters with sharp, wire prongs) are very useful for bulletin boards because of the 3-D element; and cardboard glue-on letters are useful but are somewhat less effective and durable. There are various types of press-on letters which come in sheets; these are good for small signs but care must be taken to keep the letters in even rows. There are also mechanical aids which help one to do very neat and legible lettering; a Leroy set makes pen and ink lettering almost foolproof if time is taken in learning to use it properly. Stencil lettering usually should be avoided; stencils are messy to use and the results are often uneven and unattractive. Any of these commercial letters are easier to use and reuse if they are pasted or executed on poster board strips and blocks.

Layout

Another important technical skill is layout. Layout, quite simply, is a "laying out" of shapes or design ingredients in a coherent, balanced, and effective manner. And that is what must be done with all design components: cartoons, captions, lettering strips or blocks, arrows, yarn, or whatever, Posters are usually executed on one piece of poster board and must be sketched and completely planned before any of the elements are prepared; once the board is completed it is almost impossible to make any changes in arrangement. This is not true when one is using separate design components. The layout should be planned in advance, but the layout may also be changed at any time.

Here is how layout might work in operation: suppose one wishes to make a poster on a standard piece of poster board 22 by 28 inches in size. A "thinking" cartoon and a "Check Dictionary Supplements" caption are selected, and it is decided to make the board horizontal with the 28-inch length for the width. In order to allow space for margins at the ends of the caption, the caption strip should be about 25 or 26 inches long and about 3½ or 4 inches high depending on the size of lettering used. The caption should be penciled in lightly so that one can see how it fits—if the caption is too long it will have to be changed or executed in smaller or "tighter" lettering. If, after lettering, the end margins are uneven the wider one may be trimmed off (This is one of the many advantages of separate components).

After the cartoon and caption have been placed on the board (but not affixed to it), one can determine how much space is left for the text. If, for example, four supplements are to be listed, four strips can be cut to size. The longest word or phrase can be done to establish the lettering size (and the text might have to be edited to fit the space; you often have to say what there is room for instead of exactly what you want); the other words or phrases are then centered on the other strips (or they may be done in the middle of extra long strips and then centered and trimmed the same length as the first strip). After all the strips have been lettered they can be tried on for size and balance as is shown in figure 60.

Check the margins: the edges of the lettering strips should line up with one another and possibly with the edge of the caption; the top and/or bottom of the cartoon might be in line with the top or bottom of one of the strips; the left edge of the caption could be lined up with the left edge of the cartoon and perhaps with the right edge of the strips. Figure 60 shows how

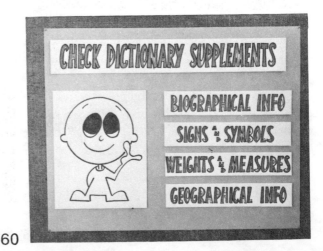

80

the pieces might be laid out; in this illustration the caption and cartoon are in line at the left, and the strips are in line at the right (they could have been pulled in tighter and lined up with the caption, but that would make the design too static); the cartoon is in line at top and bottom with the strips.

Check the contrast: do the display components stand out against the light green background or should the contrast be heightened? The strips might contrast with the background more effectively if they were set off in some way. Black rug yarn might help. In figure 61 the strips have been pulled closer together and enclosed by a yarn rectangle (and the yarn now lines up with the top and bottom of the cartoon). Perhaps the strips would show up even better glued to a piece of black poster board as has been done in figure 62 (and note that the black rectangle has been cut the same height as the cartoon). This provides even better contrast.

61

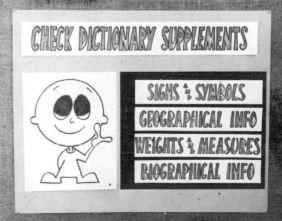

62

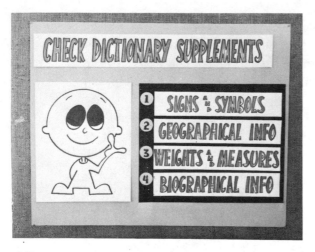

63

But the poster is still a bit dull. There may be a preponderance of rectangular shapes. Numbered green circles might help, and, as shown in figure 63, they do. Their addition, however, seemed to crowd the space between the black shape and the cartoon (additions to a design often change the balance of other elements); so the cartoon has been moved slightly to the left to make more room. And, to keep the left margin even, the caption was also moved slightly to the left.

There are other ways in which the same poster components may be used, but first it might be helpful to summarize a few points:

1. The design components should contrast effectively with the background.
2. The lettering style for the text should be uniform and the caption may be in a different, but compatible style.
3. The lettering should be penciled in so that the maximum letter size may be determined.
4. Margin lines must be considered.
5. The caption, cartoon, and text should be attached to poster board with rubber cement and to a bulletin board with map tacks.
6. All pencil lines should be erased when the poster is completed.

Next, let us examine some other possible layouts of the basic components. Figure 64 shows how the board might look without the cartoon and more contrast has been added by backing the caption with black poster board. In figure 65 the lettering strips and their black backing have been cut into strips permitting them to be spread out more. On a larger board each strip might be mounted on a large piece of poster board to fill the space even more, and the numbers might be cut off into separate pieces and used to the left or above the strips. Another possibility is to project the caption, the strips, or the numbers.

The demonstration displays were done on a board of limited size in order to point out the planning involved in designing for a specific space—how to allot space for the various elements, how to plan for margins, and how addition and subtraction of

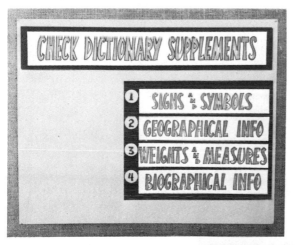

64

65

one design element affect the rest of the design. It points out the variety possible with even a small poster type display. The illustrations show only a few of the ways in which these particular elements might be used, and all of the elements can be used with other displays. For example: the caption could be used with a display directing attention to one particular section to "check" in a dictionary; the strips could be part of a quiz asking which reference source has these items, or the strips could be backed with flannel and used for a flannel board talk on dictionaries; the cartoon and numbers can be used with almost any type of display.

Cartooning

Lettering and layout are often easier to do than one might think, but cartooning presents a different problem in that it is usually more difficult than it might appear to be. However, most of the cartoons in this book are rather simple and if one has any art skill, the cartoons should not be too difficult to copy. For one with no art skill whatsoever, copying them could be an impossible task. But, no matter how lacking in talent one might be, there are cartoons which can be executed. Anyone who can trace a circle can draw a cartoon.

The first step in drawing a cartoon is to make a circle with a marking pen; a compass circle may be drawn and traced, but it is usually easier to draw around a suitably sized lid, glass, or bowl with a marker. Figure 66 shows three rows of cartoon faces; all are circles with ears added. The steps in making a basic face are shown in the first strip; add two circles for eyes; and a "U" for a nose; add a mouth; add pupils; add hair. All of the faces in the second strip are built on this basic face; the only differences are the placement of pupils, shape of the mouth, and the hair. Some variations of eyes and noses are shown in the third strip. This basic face can fill most cartooning needs with only three changes; the pupils can be moved to direct attention to another part of the design; the mouth can be smiling or frowning; and the hair can be changed or a hat may be used.

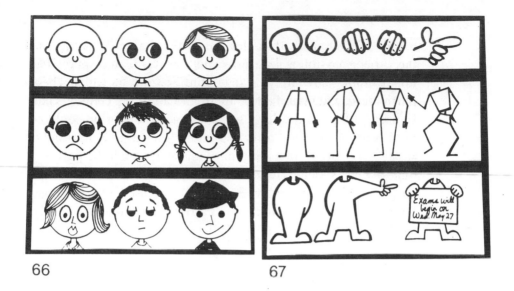

66   67

A face is the most important part of any figure cartoon, but the hands can also be very important. There are two basic uses for cartoon hands—holding and pointing; when there is nothing for them to hold or at which to point they can be hidden. The top strip of figure 67 shows a row of cartoon hands. The first two sets of hands are in a holding position; the first set is easier to make, but if one wants to be a bit more "arty" the other can be used. If these hands are cut out they can be used to hold a sign or object from the top, bottom, or sides. The last hand in the strip is pointing and it may be pointing at almost anything; a sign, lift panel, pamphlet holder, textual material, book jackets, etc.

Now that we have faces and hands, we need a body to which they can be attached. Two kinds of stick figures are shown in the middle strip of figure 67. The first type has a shoulder and hip line, and the second has a rib cage and pelvic area. These figures can be used to show movement of any kind; when showing movement the most important thing to keep in mind is that the shoulders and hips move in opposite directions; if the left shoulder is down the left hip is up, and if the right shoulder is down the right hip is tilted up. The bottom strip of figure 67 shows a different kind of body style, and this style is probably the easiest to make and the most effective. The three basic body positions are shown in this strip. Standing (with hands hidden), pointing, and holding. Figure 68 shows all of these basic cartoon faces, hands, and bodies "doing their thing."

68

VIII

IDEA SOURCES

four types of "product" approach, clientele
interest, idea file, junk box, and reference sources

This book and others in the field have many pretested display suggestions. Some of the ideas are shopworn by the time they get into print, and even if all the ideas presented were new and exciting there still would never be enough fresh ideas to meet your every display need—and it is the paucity of fresh ideas which often leads to a reliance on the tried, true, and trite standard approach (How many February displays use profile cutouts of Washington and Lincoln?). But it is the nonstandard approach which attracts attention and sells the message or product. It is necessary first of all to have a message or product to sell, and then to select a nonstandard visual presentation of the message or to add an individualizing twist to the standard approach. This is not always easy to do, but there are a number of productive idea areas; a survey of the possibilities should be helpful in the search for new solutions.

)

Product

The first area here is the product itself. A school display is seldom concerned with an actual product in the way a commercial organization might be; but any display is involved in selling something, and, to do that effectively, the "product" must be considered. The approach depends on analysis of the product and how it can be personalized and sold to a particular audience. What is it exactly that you are selling—is it an idea, event, period of history, location, technique, or specific subject? Lesson plans list not only the facts and skills which students are to learn but also the insights and understandings which (hopefully) they will acquire. These too are a part of your product and should become part of your design plan. After determining what your product is and why it is being offered, decide what there is about it that will have most appeal to your audience.

One possible area of appeal is equipment related to the subject: microscope, sewing machine, kiln, bunsen burner, abacus, compass, musical instrument, power tool, telescope, typewriter, or what you will. A large line drawing or cutout of the equipment (with parts labeled) might be featured. This drawing or cutout can be used for a variety of purposes but the information provided should be geared to the age and interest level of the expected audience. Younger students, for example, might only be interested in the fact that a microscope makes things larger, while older students would require more details on the use of the microscope or some peripheral information on the inventor or development of the instrument. Parents might be interested in what type of microscope to purchase for a child, and adults in the educational field might wish to know the sequential steps involved in a unit on use of the microscope.

Another area of interest in the product line is to display and explain some of the tools associated with different subject areas. A display of tools and machines could use large cutouts showing the difference between a claw hammer (used for driving and pulling nails) and a ball peen hammer (used for metal work) which has two striking surfaces. As the unit progresses the display can be expanded with cutouts of other tools with different uses, or to the different uses of special types of nails and screws.

A science unit could commence with an "identify the shape" quiz of test tube, beaker, clamp, and bunsen burner cutouts; a sewing display could utilize blowup drawings of different kinds of needles and their uses; a home economics exhibit might show different kinds of cookware; rock hunting tools would introduce a geology unit; a Revolutionary or Civil War unit might feature drawings, cutouts, or photographs of equipment or weapons used by the soldiers; and any unit on early America would be made more relevant with a display showing kinds of kitchen equipment, furniture, building tools, or farm tools of the period being studied.

All of these displays concerned with tools and equipment are good attention getters (especially if some real objects can be used), and, because the information is rather basic but not generally known, the same type of display can often be used for lower and upper grades and sometimes for adults. A display of this type is particularly effective educationally since it directs attention not only to an object but to the use of the object—why it was designed in a certain way and how it is used. This can be a helpful framework for explaining cause and effect relationships and in making unfamiliar subjects, periods, and techniques meaningful. Some added attractions are that a display of this type is rather easy to design; it can be used as a subject introduction; it can be expanded and used as a teaching aid; and it can be used as a culminating exhibit— especially if student-made materials are included.

A third kind of product approach is to show various techniques or materials used to accomplish similar goals. This approach can be used with arts and crafts (different tools and techniques for woodworking, sewing, enameling, pottery making, painting, drawing, sculpture, weaving, or photography); writing and literature courses (varying methods of writing a poem, telling a story, presenting an argument, reviewing a book, describing something); mathematics problems (different methods of problem solving); or with map skills (different maps of the same area).

A similar source of display ideas is to compare: old and new ways of doing something; old and current views of a person, event, or idea; or American and foreign methods and viewpoints. Comparison of dress, type of housing, literary styles, and kinds of arts and crafts can be made on either an old and new or American and foreign basis. An old and new approach might be used with map making, methods of computation, types of transportation, writing materials, or kinds of entertainment. "At the time" and current views might be applied to famous people, literary works (use *Moulton's Library of Literary Criticism†*), historical events, or social and ethical mores.

A fourth approach is people oriented—to present a subject in terms of people associated with it. History and current events are full of interesting people and information about them will often whet one's appetite for a unit of study; and, for an introduction, it is often best to concentrate on the personalities and excentricities of people. The signers of the Declaration of Independence might be introduced with a few phrases about their appearance or characters—a quiz matching names and descriptions might be used. This same technique could be used with rulers, presidents, explorers, scientists, inventors, writers, musicians, artists, generals—or just about anyone. The trick with this approach is not just to offer facts about a person but also present a few of the foibles which make him or her an individual.

The product techniques discussed have applied chiefly to displays concerned with subject areas or units of study, but similar techniques are applicable to displays dealing with peripheral materials, school activities, or educational ideas. Here too, the product must be analyzed and promoted in the most effective way possible.

†Charles W. Moulton [Martin Tucker, ed.], *Moulton's Library of Criticism of English & American Authors* (New York: Frederick Ungar Publishing Co., 1966).

Displays dealing with peripheral educational materials (current events, sports, hobbies, advanced education and training) can often employ the equipment and tools, comparison, or people-oriented approaches. If the display is continuing (the display setup is permanent but the materials change), it can be divided into interest groupings. A current events display, for example, might be divided into technological information, American and foreign press coverage of an event, or personalities in the news. Sports could be divided into materials on early types of games and competition, record holders, profiles of top teams, and personalities; education and training information might be presented by comparing different careers or different types of schools, or by discussing personalities in various fields.

The four kinds of product approach may also be used for most types of displays devoted to extracurricular school activities. A display encouraging participation in any type of activity should attempt to generate interest not only in the group but also in the subject area with which the group is concerned. Do not simply tell someone to join a club; teach them something interesting about the subject. A drama display might use drawings or photographs showing how stage make-up is applied; basic dance steps could be sketched for a dance display; a football play diagram could be explained for a sport display; and a photography club display might show a scene photographed under four different lighting conditions or at different exposure settings.

Idea displays are probably the most difficult of all to personalize, but, if they are to have any effect at all, they must be degeneralized as much as possible. "Read Books," "Don't Smoke," "Don't Drink," "Don't Get Hooked," and "Stay in School" pleas are useless unless they are supported with reasons—specific reasons which might be considered relevant by students.

If books are being sold, specific types and titles related to students' interests should be promoted; comments of students who have read and liked the books should be included if possible. A stay-in-school display could use earnings statistics of dropouts, high school and college graduates; but it would be even more relevant to students if the number of jobs, starting salaries, and training programs available locally to dropouts and graduates were compared. If students are being exhorted to avoid something potentially harmful to them, they should be offered very specific information about why it may be harmful. Perhaps the best *don't* approach is to present case studies of teenagers who *did* and wish they hadn't.

Clientele Interest

Many discussions in the book have referred to directing each display to a target audience; the emphasis, however, was on adapting display ideas to the audience. The emphasis here is on using the audience as a source for display ideas. What is happening in your city; what sports or TV shows are especially popular; what music groups are big with students; what recordings are in the top 40; what movies have caught the attention of the public? Can any of these interests be used as the basis for a display?

Local theater or dance groups might be willing to loan materials for a display. Costume and stage design sketches, lighting plans, and a prop list will show some of the pre-planning necessary for a stage production. Local artists might have some step-by-step photographs or sketches of their works to loan; local photographers might loan photographs of local scenes; a department store could provide fashion illlustrations for a display. Drawing on local resources for display ideas and materials is a technique which will be even more effective if students are able to visit the theater, studio, or store which furnished the materials.

If sports are important, bulletin boards can deal with the history of a particular sport and offer information about teams and top players in the area. Students might write sample scripts for their favorite TV shows. Students might prepare display quizzes matching TV characters and the shows in which they appear; musicians and the instruments they play or the groups to which they belong; recordings with artists; movies with writers and directors. Some of these approaches may lack real educational value but they can often serve as springboards for class discussions on related topics. The important thing is that you begin with something in which students are already interested and then extend that interest.

Many current expressions have instant appeal and these are another audience-generated idea source. Such expressions may be related to a single activity such as sports or music, or they may be all-purpose. Some of the all-purpose expressions which have been used extensively are "Would You Believe," "Tell It Like It Is," "Come Where It's Happening," "Groovy," "Rap," and so forth. Used as captions, these expressions are good attention grabbers and can be used for a variety of displays. However they must be up to date; don't use "Try for an Extra Point" when it is baseball season and don't use any all-purpose expression which is dated. The best way to find out what's in is to ask a teenager.

Idea File

A third productive source of ideas is an idea file. Any interesting, clever, unusual, or particularly well-drawn cartoon or drawing should be clipped from newspapers, magazines (not from current library copies of course), and publishers' and supply house catalogs. It is unnecessary to have specific use in mind for the clipping; anything which attracts attention should be clipped and put into a folder. When an idea is needed, just sorting through the folder may be helpful. Cartoon characters could be used with captions such as "Did You Hear," "Is It True," "Will Mr. Bowen Really Do It" (start a new unit) "Come Where It's Happening" (in the science lab), or "Make the Scene." Cartoons of people and animals can be saying almost anything, and they can carry signs or point to signs.

If a similar cartoon can be executed, or if someone can be located to do it, most of the problem is solved. No copyrighted cartoon or cartoon character may be reproduced without permission of the copyright holder, but it is usually acceptable to use similar cartoons for bulletin boards or for posters which will not be reproduced. If your cartoon is copied from a comic strip or from the work of a cartoonist with a highly individual style, it is best to make some acknowledgement of the source. If, for example, you use a character from Peanuts on a bulletin board, you might add a note at the bottom: "With apologies to Charles Schulz."

If no one is available to draw a similar cartoon, the caption suggested by the cartoon clipping might be sufficient by itself. The clipping file should be constantly expanded, and nothing should be discarded once it has been used; many of the same ideas may be used over and over again with only a slight variation or sometimes none at all. Your school may provide paraprofessional or student help for classroom displays, and if so cartoons from the file can be of great assistance in helping decide what is needed in the way of art work and in explaining the needs to your helper.

Junk Box

A fourth source of ideas is a junk box; the size and type of junk saved will depend on the available space and one's packrat talent. Junk collected might include pieces of fabric and wood, old keys, used batteries and flash bulbs, cord, broken eyeglasses, travel brochures, phonograph records, pieces of clothing, broken toys—just about anything which might possibly be used for future display. As with the cartoons, one need have no particular use in mind; that comes later.

Some of the things you might do with the junk are:

Cover half a bulletin board with old flashlight batteries and use captions such as "Power Up with a Balanced Diet" (or with "good study habits," "this selection of books") or "You'll Need Extra Energy for the Dance" (the track season, the new science unit, the paper drive).

Cover a large area with playing cards and use "It's in the Cards ... that this will interest you" or "Tell Your Own Future" (with a display of vocational materials).

Use rows of paper plates with "Fill Them Up at the Banquet" or "We're Serving Political Issues" (or "Thoughts to Chew on," "Tidbits About People").

Use light bulbs with "Brighten Your Knowledge" (in some particular area) or "Light Up Your Reading Interest."

Glue paper money to poster board to sell a unit on the stock market, consumer education, or business.

Displays of this kind are limited only by the imagination (which can be stretched with use), and little art work is required other than the caption.

These miscellaneous scrap items may also be combined with cartoon figures or poster board cutouts. Cartoon figures can be wearing hats, neckties, handkerchiefs, buttons or bows, jewelry, and items of clothing. A cartoon figure might be holding a fistful of play money, a travel brochure, a paper plate, or a sign; it might be leaning against a sign, a real board fence, or a wall (stone or brick-textured paper or vinyl) or sitting on a box, a fence, a tightrope, a board teeter-totter, or a step ladder made of scrap wood. Some possible uses of scrap materials with cutouts are mentioned in chapter VI. The cartoons, cutouts, and the junk should be saved for reuse either separately or together.

Miscellaneous Sources

A fifth idea area is the very broad one of professional books, pamphlets, magazines, and of reference sources. Materials dealing directly with displays must be included among these idea sources—but only to the extent that you are able to use the materials as *idea sources* rather than patterns to duplicate. Many books and pamphlets deal with teaching techniques and ideas; some offer a wide range of ideas and others concentrate on a single area of the curriculum. Some of the ideas presented deal with displays but more original ideas can be culled from the tips and tricks for teaching the different subjects. If you find a new subject approach exciting, it is not too difficult to translate the approach into display terms.

The same holds true for professional magazines. Check the

display articles for ideas but concentrate even more on the display possibilities of suggested subject approaches; some of the enrichment ideas offered are naturals for displays. Another excellent source of ideas are magazines for children which are often full of visual games and puzzles. Since the drawings are simplified for communication at a child's level there is little visual translation required in adapting them to a display.

Reference sources can yield a plethora of display ideas. Go to the reference section of your library, browse, and take notes. Start with an unabridged dictionary: flip through it and make note of any full page color plates which might be adapted for displays (different birds, flags, butterflies, flowers, weather symbols); then check the supplements for ideas for quiz displays (brief information on people, places, events, list of presidents, weights and measures, distances between cities).

Some of the most famous quotations come from unexpected sources: use a book of familiar quotations to collect material. Check *The Book of the Presidents, Current Biography, Who's Who* (and other biographical sources) for people information; use *Famous First Facts, Book of the Days,* and almanacs and books of facts for off-beat but interesting ideas. Trace historical maps or make photocopies of battlefield scenes from an historical atlas; use plot synopses from *Masterplots* and have students match them with titles; photocopy reviews of famous books from *Book Review Digest* or *Moulton's Library of Literary Criticism,* mark out the titles, and have the students guess the author or title.

Most important of all, use encyclopedias. Just flip through and see what the illustrations have to suggest. Some illustrations you might wish to copy (or to have copied) but many times the illustrations will suggest a different display approach. Illustrations of musical instruments may suggest a display using similar materials, but it may also suggest a display without drawings—such as one matching names of instruments with their family groups of woodwinds, brass, or percussion.

It is a good idea to look through all the encyclopedias in your library and see which present the most ideas in the most usuable manner. Photographs, for example, are difficult to copy in detail unless they are unusually sharp. Line drawings, however, are easy to adapt for display use and *World Book* is particularly generous with these. With whichever encyclopedia you prefer, the ideas are distilled for you in full-page illustrations, special sections, and unusual approaches. It takes little search to uncover the ideas and little more to adapt them for displays.

PUTTING IT ALL TOGETHER

step-by-step illustration and discussion of
how sample displays are designed and executed

The previous chapters discussed various aspects of display work—goals and methods of using audiovisual materials, special functions of displays, varieties of form, design elements and principles, execution and use of design components, art techniques, and idea sources. For purpose of discussion it was necessary to disassemble displays and present step-by-step explanations of the importance and purpose of each aspect of display planning and execution. Now that we have examined the individual pieces, we will reassemble some displays (figures 69 through 74 show some examples) to see how all the pieces fit together.

Suppose, for example, that one wishes to arrange a bulletin board display for music month. One standard solution is to show a few dancing notes with the caption "It's Music Month." This does direct attention to the existence of music month, but it does not deal with the real crux of the problem—the offering of musical information in graphic form. Goals must be specific. It should be determined *what* information will be offered, *how* it will be presented, and *why* (and "because it's music month" is not sufficient in itself). Selection of specific educational goals and appropriate materials is always a problem, but it is even more difficult when dealing with a broad subject area. It is often helpful, however, to consider the various possibilities before making a final selection.

Chapter VIII covered idea sources for displays. One idea approach mentioned was presenting a display in terms of tools and equipment, in this case, musical instruments. The first problem with this approach is availability of materials. Displaying real instruments would be the most effective solution, but instruments are too expensive and too heavy to tack up on a bulletin board (though use of display cases might be feasible for a different type of display). Other possibilities are use of photographs or drawings of instruments, and, if these materials are available, it must be decided if they are of a size and quality which are suitable for display purposes.

Other possibilities are to consider the product in terms of old and new or American and foreign viewpoints, or to present it using a "people" approach. It is relatively easy to hear differences in music, but it is another matter to present these differences visually; here too, however, one might use instruments of other periods and countries to point out cultural and technical variations. A people-oriented presentation could center on performers, conductors, or composers, and a display of this type for students might include a few pop or jazz stars. These types of displays could be arranged in series (perhaps using positive-negative backgrounds) with a cumulative display, possibly in quiz form, at the end of the month.

Clientele interest is an idea approach which can be used here. If some students are jazz buffs, they could be asked to help prepare a quiz matching jazz artists with their instruments, or jazz composers with their works. The same approach can be taken with classical compositions, operas, and Broadway shows; composers can be matched with works, singers with roles, and characters with the operas or musicals.

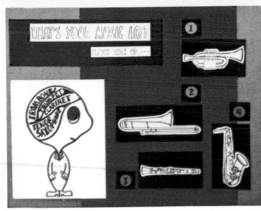

69

70

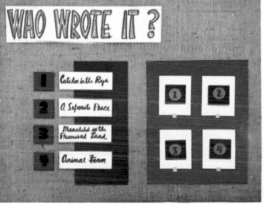

71

72

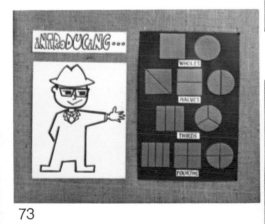

73

74

If the school has a band or orchestra, another client approach would be to present a display centering on the cost of various instruments and the relative difficulty in learning to play them.

Cartoons and objects are good attention getters, and they are also idea-suggestive gimmicks; cartoons often suggest captions and cartoon figures might be playing broken or discarded toys—harmonica, guitar, bugle, drum, or xylophone. Be sure, however, not to stop with the gimmick; use the gimmick to get attention and then proceed to the educational purpose. You might, for example, label the parts on the toy guitar, or disassemble the toy guitar to show the construction. The display might include mention of kinds of wood used in guitar making, or construction differences between a western and a Spanish guitar. A cartoon figure holding rythym blocks or a toy drum could direct attention to different types of percussion instruments used throughout the world, and a figure holding a bugle could introduce brass instruments in the orchestra.

Display pamphlets and reference sources are possible sources of ideas. Many of the ideas in display pamphlets rely on gimmicks alone for this type of peripheral display (peripheral in the sense that this display may not be part of a classroom unit of study), but some of the ideas may be helpful if they are expanded. Check the music articles in encyclopedias. Some have excellent articles on history of music, music in other countries, line drawings of musical instruments, and some show diagrams of arrangements of instruments in an orchestra. The articles furnish concise background information, and, since they are written from an interest point of view, they can help generate ideas. The line drawings can be copied, and arrangements of orchestra instruments can be used for a display requiring no "art" work (colored circles can represent the musicians, and students can match the different colors with a list of sections in the orchestra).

Now that we have covered some of the idea possibilities, let us summarize some of the other factors involved. The choice of content depends on the background and interest of the students, availability of material, and the production quality of the material. Material used for students with little musical exposure and for musically sophisticated students *may* be the same (both groups might be interested in "popular" instruments or instruments from other countries and cultures) but the approach will be different. What is displayed depends, of course, on what is available. You might have access to photographs of students playing orchestra instruments. Fine. But are the photographs large enough to be used for a bulletin board display, are they of good quality, and is the clothing worn in the photographs still in style? Perhaps students in the school have made wire sculptures of instruments and musicians; these might be suitable for an art display but they may be too abstract for a display dealing specifically with music. Any materials must be carefully scrutinized; the mere fact of availability and relationship to the subject of the display does not mean that the materials are appropriate.

If suitable materials are not available, some must be obtained. It may not be necessary to purchase study prints or make original drawings, but research may be required. A display may require blocks of lettering on instruments, musical history, or people; and a teacher may have to research and execute these, or supervise the work of paraprofessionals or students who do it. Students may be willing and able to make drawings of instruments (they might use the opaque projector to enlarge encyclopedia drawings which can then be traced), but, here too, the production quality is important. Drawings should be well done, large enough to be seen at a distance, and executed with a marking pen on poster board. Then, once the basic materials are assembled, they must be arranged according to design principles.

After considering idea and material possibilities, the educational uses of these ideas and materials must be considered. If the display is to be an introduction to a subject, it may be sufficient to pique interest or curiosity.

A quiz can do this by nudging students to check on their own knowledge. A student may not recognize the shapes of different instruments or know their "family" names, and calling this to their attention may make them more receptive to a class discussion on the subject. Students may be interested in how and why African tribes make and use musical instruments and how they fit into the total culture of the tribe. In this case, the display may be an introduction of a new unit of study, or, if African culture has already been studied, the display will extend the learning that has already taken place. A take-apart instrument display will show cause and effect relationships—how a guitar or other instrument is designed and constructed to produce a certain sound.

In most instances the purpose or purposes of a display should be determined (at least tentatively) before sorting through possible approaches; the educational purpose should influence the selection of display ideas rather than the other way around. For this particular display, however, the general theme was already established—music month—and sometimes it is necessary to consider the idea and material possibilities before selecting an appropriate educational goal. Even when the educational purpose is decided first, it can be modified to fit in with available materials or the particular interests of students. But, whichever selection sequence is used, educational purpose, suitability of materials, and student interest are all factors which must be considered.

We will now select a purpose (to introduce a subject), translate it into visual form (use drawings of instruments), and select a display form (a bulletin board). The next step is to execute the display in terms of design principles. Figure 75 shows the basic ingredients: marking-pen sketches of four musical instruments and strips of poster board with names of the instruments. In figure 76 a caption and subcaption have

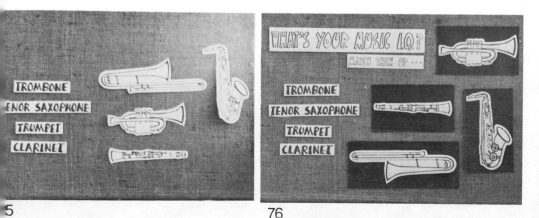

been added and the instruments have been mounted on black poster board. The backings make the drawings easier to handle and more durable (they were executed on rather flimsy paper); they add unity since all the blocks are the same width; and they add contrast. The ingredients are now ready but design principles are still lacking.

Figure 77 shows how the ingredients are pulled into a design unit with only slight shifting. The name strips have been moved to line up with the left edge of the caption, and the longest strip was placed at the bottom to furnish a "heavier" bottom margin (the trombone was moved up to make room for the longer bottom strip). The black blocks were shifted to make even margins on the top, bottom, and right side; some of the blocks line up to make an internal margin. In figure 78 small red circle numbers have been added; these are a bright addition to the design and will make it easier to furnish answers to the quiz. In figure 79 the design is improved still more with the addition of a matching red strip of construction paper.

Now let us move the same ingredients to a larger bulletin board (figure 80) and see how the arrangement looks. It looks too small. But these are the components we have to work with, and, short of redoing them, what can be done? One of the things which can be done is to fill the space and figure 81 shows one way of doing this. The space has been filled with large simple shapes and no clutter has been added. The caption and strips have been backed with poster board and a large background piece helps pull the isolated elements together.

Horn 1 now lines up with the bottom of the caption, and, since the background shape creates a strong right margin, horn 4 juts through the margin slightly to add interest. Now look at the difference between figures 80 and 81; the changes have been simple (no dancing notes or bars of music were tossed in), but they have changed a too small, blah design into an effective bulletin board display. Another display possibility is shown in figure 82. One of the cartoon captions is used as a space filling, interest grabber; another change is that the small

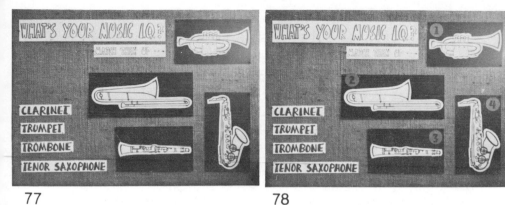

77

78

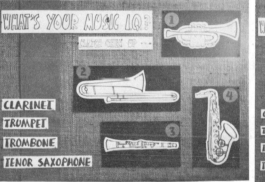

79

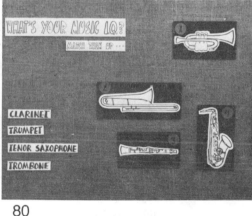

80

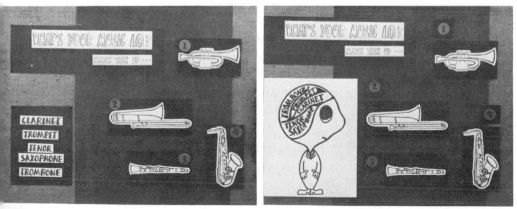

81

82

red numbers have been glued to black squares. The squares may now be moved around to make different patterns; in figure 82 the pattern is rather scattered, but in figure 69 they have been shifted somewhat to provide a tighter right angle design. This use of numbers on separate blocks or circles of poster board can be a logical, space filling, and effective addition to many different displays.

The problem now is to evaluate the display in terms of goals and materials; did the display do what it was supposed to do and were the materials selected appropriate? Did students look at the display; how many students looked at the answers (which should be posted nearby); when the subject was discussed in class how many students could identify the instruments (and how many students indicated that they had not known the instruments before looking at the display)? Was the quiz too easy, too hard, or inappropriate for the audience? If most of the students were familiar with the instruments, then perhaps the display should have asked which were brass and which woodwinds.

Were the materials appropriate? Were the materials large enough, well done, and did they fulfill the educational purpose for which they were intended? The original materials were not really large enough or sturdy enough, but black backings compensated for this deficiency; they were visible and were of adequate quality for display purposes. Since the educational purpose was only to indicate the shapes of the horns, the materials did fulfill the educational purpose. However, if the display had dealt with instrument design, the materials would not have been adequate since the drawings are not accurately detailed. Were some students critical of this lack of detail? If students are sufficiently knowledgeable to notice the lack, then the drawings might be inappropriate for this particular audience—though educational purposes are well served if students are concerned enough to locate or make better drawings.

An added evaluative criterion which always figures in any display is whether or not the display materials can be reused.

Displays require time, energy, and planning and it is inefficient (and frustrating) to set up a display which will be thrown away in its entirety. All of these materials are durable and adaptable. The instruments can be added to and used for displays teaching instrument families; each instrument and its history may be presented in separate displays; instruments may be used with orchestra plans (rug yarn may be stretched from each drawing to its place in the orchestra), and, if students are interested in jazz, they may use the instruments to set up displays showing the composition of famous jazz groups.

The caption and subcaption may be used with some of these displays or with others—perhaps with a "composers and their works" series on a positive-negative display board. The numbers and cartoon figure may be used for a variety of displays. The instruments may be used for announcement displays. A cartoon figure holding a horn could announce a school dance or band recital. He could be saying "We're blowing our own horn" about a special event, or "We don't want to horn in" or "Get in step."

Figure 70 shows a small display which is not sturdy enough for a bulletin board display, but which will make an effective classroom teaching aid. The design of a teaching aid differs somewhat from a display which must exist independently; a teaching aid will be used as a lecture or discussion aid and it may list only key words or phrases which will then be explained on the spot.

It is used as a prop to focus student attention. The aid shown in figure 70 uses two circles, one smaller in diameter than the other, a map tack pivot, and a small rubber washer with which to "dial" the desired section. This particular display is divided into four segments and the information will be changed for each state. You may, of course, use as many or as few divisions as you wish, so long as the information is large enough to be seen by the class. This same type of presentation may be used for different countries, kinds of plants and animal life, people associated with a period, event, or profession—or with any study which can be separated into segments. Once the

83

discs are made, one only needs to change the information to be "dialed" as it is discussed.

Figure 83 shows a quiz matching four authors and titles (the titles are from a college reading list). The authors and titles were written with a marking pen on separate strips of poster board; they were attached to the background pieces with glue (rubber cement was used so that the pieces could easily be peeled off and replaced). The background is designed with three identical blocks of black poster board, one of which has a lift panel attached. Since the background is very static, design interest is added by having the lettering strips "stick off" to the side.

A different set-up is shown in figure 84; only the titles are used and a lift panel board has each answer under a separate panel (this type of board is made by taping—from underneath—four small pieces of poster board to a larger piece). The panel numbers are an attractive design device, and they too are attached with rubber cement so they may be peeled off and used for other displays (You may notice that these are the same numbers used on the music display). In figure 71 another set of numbers has been added; these are cutout numbers glued to squares of poster board which are then map tacked to the bulletin board. These numbers add little to the function of the display but they do contribute to the effectiveness of the design.

108

A similar display with a different type of lift panel is shown in figure 85. The lift panel board in this figure is made from one piece of poster board; four rectangles were cut out entirely (if the tops had been bent rather than cut and taped, the panels would stick out rather than lying flat). The panels shown are attached with masking tape, but one might use any kind or color of plastic tape desired. The panel board in figures 84 and 71 requires separate answers glued or tacked under each panel; with the display shown in figure 85, however, all the answers may be on one sheet of paper placed behind the panel board. The lift panel boards may be used with just a caption to make a smaller display; if the "Who Wrote It?" caption were used, small title strips could be glued to the panels. The panel board may, of course, be made much larger and as few or as many lifts as desired may be used.

84

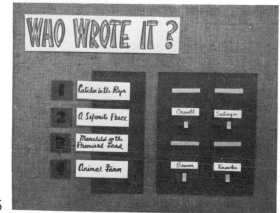

85

A display of this type requires very little time for preparation of materials, and, once the lift panels and caption are made, even less time is necessary to sustain the display. Whole series of books and authors may be used (or artists and paintings, musicians and compositions, people and events) and only the title and author pieces need to be changed.

The display may be used to direct attention to works which will be studied in class, works which have been studied, or to direct students to outside reading. The matching materials may be selected by the teacher (for an introduction) or by the students (for a culminating display); a compromise system would be for the teacher to select display items from student reports. This type of board might be used to direct attention to another board displaying relevant student reports. An art and artists board could be combined with a display of prints; and events and dates would tie in with an exhibit of appropriate historical maps.

Encyclopedia sections on animals offer many useful ideas such as the one shown in figure 86. This particular idea is based on a chart showing the relative speed of animals on land and in water (other adaptable ideas are ways in which different animals move and tracks of different animals). Four animals were chosen for the display and simple sketches were made on blocks of poster board. The drawings are small (they occupy only about 10 percent of the display space) so a space filling arrangement was necessary, and a simple background of three green rectangles was used. The idea of a race seemed an effective way of attracting attention and materials were arranged with this in mind. The sketches were first arranged

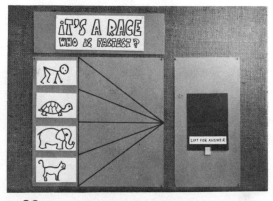

on a "straight" track, and, while the arrangement was acceptable, it was rather dull.

The triangular track was tried out next and this added variety and also served to direct attention to the lift panel. The design was jazzed up somewhat (but not necessarily improved) with the addition of black and white triangles shown in figure 72. The L-shaped arrow was also added, and it provides added contrast and extra emphasis on the lift panel. In place of a lift panel one might use a small block of poster board listing the order of finish (at 30 mph, the cat wins).

Any display dealing with the speed or movement of animals would be a good introduction to adaptation of animals to their environment and how animals defend themselves. The display could emphasize this still further by directing attention to the difference between land and water speed of the same animals. This type of exhibit would be more interesting in the lower grades if student drawings were used, and if students chose which animals to "race," and then guessed at the probable results of such a race.

The display in figure 87 was suggested by a pamphlet on development of map reading skills. The display may be used as an introduction to a unit, and it could be added to and used as a developmental and cumulative display. Each point of information can be displayed before and during the time it is being studied, and then all the "skills" (which should be mounted on the same size poster board) can be combined in a cumulative display which could be coordinated with a map or

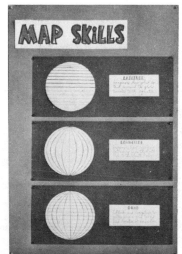

globe. If the poster board blocks are backed with a nappy fabric, they will serve double duty as flannel board teaching aids.

Figures 73 and 74 both employ a cartoon figure as an attention and space filling device. Figure 73 is based on an idea from a pamphlet on teaching mathematics, and it could introduce a whole series of math concepts. The display in figure 74 is from an idea in a children's magazine and it might present a series of foreign words. The materials in all the displays should be saved for reuse elsewhere.

If you look through the illustrations in this chapter, you will see how the design elements of color, line, shape, texture, and space have been used in accord with the principles of simplicity, emphasis, unity, and balance. The colors and shapes used have been extremely simple. All of the displays use only one color, tan, white, and in some displays black; the displays have only rectangles, circles, and triangles (The directional shape in figure 72 is, geometrically, two rectangles and a triangle). Margin lines, both internal and external, are carefully considered in each display, and figure 86 makes strong use of line to provide emphasis. The textured bulletin board background takes care of that element nicely and its use provides automatic contrast with the other elements. The use of any element against a background shape provides automatic spatial relationship (the element on top is "in front" of the other) and overlapping lettering strips in figures 79 and 83); use of lift panels provides additional space interest.

The displays discussed have all been based on teacher-prepared materials and the ideas have come from a variety of sources. Each of the displays shown could be executed in an almost infinite variety of ways and there would be no one "right" way. All that the illustrations have shown are a few of the possibilities which can be developed from simple ideas—by using a few simple elements and principles—and by adhering to a few simple guidelines. But then anything is simple once you know how. Even display work.

Appendix

TECHNICAL INFORMATION

Keep in mind that all construction methods discussed are very simple even though the directions may, at times, seem complicated. The possible complication of the directions is an attempt to anticipate any difficulties which you might have in following the procedures or in explaining them to others. How-to-do-it whizzes may find some of the information superfluous, but the details are for the non-whizzes who might prefer too much information to too little.

Bulletin Boards

Bulletin board construction is the only task to be discussed which requires elaborate equipment—that is if one considers a hammer, a saw, and a stapler elaborate equipment. Also requires are a few 1- or 2-inch nails (almost any kind except small headed finishing nails), a few small eye screws (screws with a closed loop at one end) and hook screws (ones with a hook at one end), and some long strips of $\frac{3}{4} \times 1\frac{1}{2}$-inch wood (or similar size). Naturally one also needs bulletin board material and the most useful type is soft fiberboard. This type of board is cheaper than the lowest grade plywood (which is too hard and too heavy for bulletin boards) and it is available in a variety of sizes and thicknesses—the thickness is relatively unimportant as long as it is at least ½ inch. Fiberboard is sold under a variety of names depending on the construction use for which it is intended, and, also depending on use, it may be unfinished or have one painted surface, usually white.

Soundproofing panels are painted white and the largest size available is usually 2 feet by 4 feet; some panels are textured so it is best to request a smooth surface variety. Insulating sheathing is another type of fiberboard; it may be painted and is usually available in 4-feet by 8-feet sheets. The building supply company from which the sheets are purchased may cut them to your measurements, but, if not, the board is easily cut with almost any type of saw. It can even be deeply scored with a heavy duty knife and then broken along the cut.

If the bulletin boards are to be painted, it is best to purchase fiberboard with one finished surface since a raw surface will absorb too much paint. In order to avoid glare, flat, nonglossy paint is used; the edge of the board may be painted the same color or black. If a more finished edge is desired, narrow strips of wood edging or moulding may be glued and/or nailed around the board (since nails will not hold too well in the soft fiberboard, it is usually best to use both glue and nails). Moulding attached in this way is not true framing and the moulding will not support the weight of the board; it is used only for a finished appearance. Correct framing is expensive, heavy, and is not really necessary for bulletin boards.

A better solution than painting is to cover the boards with a rough textured fabric such as burlap; the fabric is simply pulled tightly around the board and stapled to the back (stretch burlap over an unfinished side of board so that paint will not show through the loose weave of the material). This provides an attractive, textured surface which will not get the pock marked effect of painted boards, and which will show off smooth surfaced display materials. An added advantage to use of burlap covering is that the edges of the fiberboard are covered and protected, eliminating the need for any type of moulding.

If school hallways and classrooms are already bright, natural burlap can be used; a tan background contrasts effectively with black, white, and almost all colors used against it. Burlap is available in a wide range of decorator colors which can give drab or uninteresting hallways or class-rooms a whole new look. Three side by side boards (perhaps 2-feet by 4-feet boards hung vertically) might be in primary colors; in lime, green, and blue; or in various shades of red and orange. For greater unity, all the boards in one room could be the same color, with, perhaps, one board in a complementary color. The choice is wide and the price is cheap. An extra attraction which has been mentioned previously is that burlap is nappy enough to be used for flannel board displays; display materials backed with felt or flannel will stick to burlap (they will only "stick" temporarily, so must be tacked down for a lasting display). This means that any flannel backed teaching aid can be "stuck," as it is discussed, on any board in the class-room. This is a simple technique but it looks like magic to students.

If your bulletin board is used on an easel, nothing more needs to be done. If it is to be attached to a wall, there are several options which should be considered. The fiberboard, whether burlap covered or moulding edged, may be nailed directly to the wall; this is the simpler method. The board may be "hung" on the wall, and that is the preferred method though it does involve a few extra steps. Fiberboard is too soft to hold screws, so a strip of wood should be nailed to the back of the board and screws secured in the wood. As shown in figure 88, the wood strip is shorter than the width of the board and is attached near the top. Two or three nails are driven through the front of the fiberboard into the wood strip; if the nail points protrude they are simply pounded over. Eye screws are then attached at each end of the wood strip. The board in figure 88 was covered with burlap before the strip was

88

attached, but it is usually better to cover the board afterwards in order to cover the nail heads on the front of the board (be sure to make the wood strip short enough to allow room for stapling the burlap to the back of the board).

The next consideration is a place to hang the board. The eye screws on the back of the board may be hung on protruding nails or on hook screws attached directly to a wall. If the composition of the wall will not hold nails or screws, it is usually possible to attach a strip of wood to the wall and then screw the hooks into the wood. One advantage to this indirect attachment is that the board can be laid flat while a design arrangement is tried out; when the layout is satisfactory the materials can be tacked down and the board rehung.

An added advantage to this type of arrangement is that bulletin boards can be moved from one location to another. If all classroom boards are 4 feet by 4 feet and eye screws and hook screws are the same distance apart, all the boards will be interchangeable. Since the boards are unframed and therefore very light in weight, most boards may be moved by one person with no difficulty (no rush calls for the maintenance crew). An introductory display can be hung on one of the back boards and then shifted up front when the unit gets underway. A Lincoln display can be in the back of the room during the early part of February and then moved up for his birthday. A particularly successful display of student hobbies can be moved to a more prominent position for a few days and then moved to the side or rear area again. An "in progress" display can stay on a back board until it is finished and then moved to its more permanent location. This shifting of bulletin boards around a classroom insures maximum exposure for all displays and creates a continually fresh appearance in the classroom (students never know what board they will be looking at each day), and no extra effort is involved.

To carry the idea even further, if classrooms, hallways, and the library all had at least a few standard size boards and attachments, any classroom display could be moved to the hallway, to the library, or to another classroom—and visa versa. This type of bulletin board traffic can be exciting for students since their own displays reach a wider audience, and they, in turn, are exposed to displays done in the library or in other classrooms. This also helps alleviate the "who does the hallway bulletin board" problem. Classroom and library displays will always be on tap for hallway use, and they will usually be more valid educationally than the decorative displays one often finds there (as hallway displays, they will be more significant educationally if the teacher adds a brief critique as to the purpose and achievement of the unit). The classroom-to-hall bulletin board bit is particularly great for PTA, school board meetings, and open house; it is an effective way to show your educational wares.

Pamphlet Holders

Schools often receive pamphlets of various kinds and their distribution can be a problem. Pamphlet holders are a solution: holders keep the materials together; having the pamphlets "up" rather than spread on a table assures more attention; and holders can be a versatile and attractive display ingredient. Holders are easy to make, use, and store. Figure 89

117

shows the cutting and assembly pattern of one basic type; the front and back are the same size, and the sides, bottom, and two attaching pieces are the same size. The construction paper is folded on the dotted lines; the front folded up, the sides around, and the attaching pieces are glued or stapled in place. A "quickie" holder is shown in figure 90; this is simply a folded piece of construction paper with colored tape around the top. Holders can be made any color and can be decorated with a geometric marking pen design. To allow for easy reuse of the holders, the best method is to glue them to larger pieces of poster board which can then be attached to a bulletin board and removed and stored after use.

Shelves

Figure 91 shows the cutting and folding pattern, and the mounting of one type of simple shelf. The angled support piece

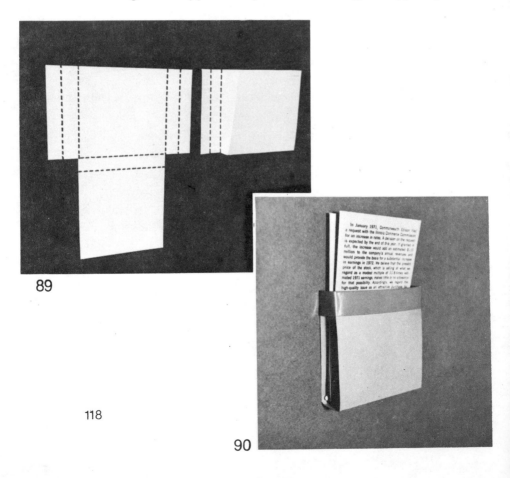

89

90

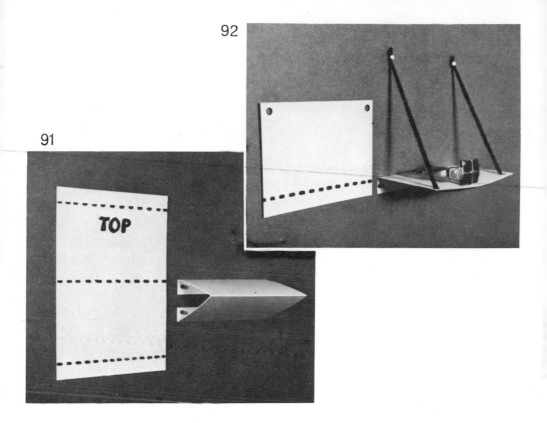

is slightly wider than the top of the shelf, and the two attaching pieces are the same size and are folded under and tacked or stapled to the board. The shelf can be made of any size and color poster board; it is rather sturdy (strong enough to support paperback books, small sculptures, rock samples, and so forth); and it can be removed and used again.

A different type of shelf is pictured in figure 92. This is a one-fold shelf with two punched holes through which wire or yarn can be strung. The folded support is attached to the board, then, as shown in the illustration, yarn is strung through the holes and the ends tacked to the board. This type of shelf is not as sturdy as the other and will sag slightly under weight. Both of these shelves are of poster board, and when folding poster board (for this or other projects) it is best to score it very lightly with a sharp knife or razor, and then bend it back along the cut.

93

94

Three-Dimensional Devices

There are numerous methods of adding three-dimensional elements to displays and two of them are shown in figures 93 and 94. Figure 93 shows a poster board caption with two folded flaps at each end—one fold for depth and one for attachment. The attaching flap is tacked or stapled to the bulletin board, or glued to the sign or poster, and, viola, the caption projects. A different method is shown in figure 94. Here the poster board is folded into a small open box which is attached to the board, rolled masking tape, sticky side out, or foam tape attach the caption to the front of the box. For long captions, two boxes of the same depth would be required at each end of the caption. Real boxes may also be used. An end opening box would be tacked to the board and the caption attached with tape. A box with a top is separated, the bottom attached to the board; rolled masking tape, sticky side out, or foam tape attach the caption to the front of the box. For long may be used with any display components—blocks of text, cartoons, pamphlet holders, or cutouts.

120

Reproduction Technique

There are many times when it is useful to have copies of cartoons or other display components, and though many schools lack printing equipment they do have photocopy machines. The maximum size for many of these machines is 8½ by 13 inches which is rather small for most purposes. But there are possibilities. Figure 95 shows a basic cartoon figure which has been squeezed into an 8½ by 13-inch format; in figure 96 the cartoon pieces have been cut out, stretched to an 18-inch high figure, and mounted on poster board. The hands are hinged from underneath with tape so that they project somewhat. These figures may be drawn, reproduced, and used as sign holding devices throughout the school, or they may be given a name and become class mascots. Mr. "Bippy"—or three or four Mr. Bippys in a row—might hold book jackets, book reports, themes, study prints, pamphlets, or anything you can think of. He can have different expressions, hairstyles, hats, or clothing.

Other cartoons and cutouts may be reproduced a piece at a time, and then reassembled. The same technique may be used with captions; each word may be run off separately and then reassembled on a colored strip of poster board. Blocks of text may be reproduced in the same way.

95   96

Attachment

Let me first state that I am highly prejudiced in favor of map tacks for most bulletin board purposes. Map tacks are small enough to be very unobtrusive at a distance, especially if they are the same color as the material on which they are used, and they are an attractive addition when they are seen. They are longer than thumb tacks and will therefore hold better if they must attach several layers of poster board or other material. They do not scar any material which they attach; they leave only a small hole. Map tacks are available in a wide range of colors and may be either the same color as the display material or a contrasting color. They are not usually available at variety stores but are sold at most office supply companies. Buy them and use them.

Thumb tacks are not designed for use on bulletin boards. The top is large so they may be pushed or driven into a hard surface and then pried up for removal; the shank is too short to hold several layers of material. The profusion of little "spots" all over a display is distracting; even if the tacks are a matching color they shine and create glare spots. An added liability is that the top makes scars; it leaves round indentations, and often stains, which make it difficult to reuse the display material.

Staples are less obtrusive than thumb tacks but use of too many produces a metalic shine which detracts from the effectiveness of the display. They may be used on the back folds of captions and shelves or the backs of pamphlet holders; however, since they also scar and stain surfaces, they should not be affixed to the front of material which you want to reuse. They are useful for assembly of various materials and for temporary attachment of materials which are to be discarded after use.

Transparent tape should never be used to attach anything—even temporarily—to a bulletin board or poster. The tape shines, it turns brown very quickly, and it ruins the surface of the material which it is attaching. It may be rolled, sticky side out, and used on the back of something to attach it

122

temporarily, but masking tape usually holds better used in this way (transparent tape with two sticky surfaces may also be used in this way, but it is rather difficult to work with). When tape is needed to hold materials together or for a hinge (as with lift panels), it is best to use colored plastic tape which holds as well and looks better.

Foam tape is adhesive on both sides, will hold heavier materials than other tapes, and is very useful for attaching poster board signs or posters to walls, metal and wood surfaces. It cannot, however, be removed from poster board or paper without tearing off some of the surface; therefore it should not be used on bulletin boards except to attach cartoons or captions to boxes or for materials which cannot be attached in any other way.

Also available is a soft putty which is rolled into small balls and used on the back of material to be attached. It is not terribly adhesive but it may be used for temporary layouts which will then be tacked into place. If left in place too long, it may pull off part of the poster board surface when removed and it may leave a greasy stain, especially on poster board or paper.

Rubber cement is particularly useful for attaching pieces of paper or poster board together. Any excess can simply be "rolled off" when it dries and it leaves no stain. If used on only one of the surfaces to be attached, it is often possible to separate the pieces without damaging either surface. For more permanent attachment both surfaces should be coated, allowed to dry, and then put together. Other types of paste and glue may also be used, but both pieces will probably be damaged when they are separated (and "wet" glues often warp the paper which they attach).

Potpourri

One of the most important things in using separate display components is to see that all components are cut with perfectly straight edges. Even carefully done scissor cutting leaves a slightly rippled edge which detracts from the display; therefore one should use either a paper cutter, or cut with a sharp knife or razor along a metal edged ruler. If students are too young to handle this type of cutting, the teacher or an aid should do it for them. Another thing to remember is that components which are to be the same size, must be the same size—not almost the same size. And components which are to be evenly spaced must not be "almost" evenly spaced. Attention to these seemingly minor details can often make the difference between a successful display and one which is "almost" successful.

Index

Aesthetic functions of displays, 7-8, 24-25

Administrators, as display audience, 21, 23-24

Alignment of materials in displays, 45-46, 80-84, 104-106

Analogous color harmony, 42

Artistic ability. See Skills required for display work; Techniques for display work

Attachment of display materials, 13, 29, 31, 82, 108, 118, 120, 122-123

Audiences, specialized, for displays administrators, 21, 23-24
board of trustees, 22
faculty and staff, 20-21, 28, 88
parents, 12-13, 21-22, 55, 88
public, 28, 55

Audiovisuals, 4-6
educational values, 5
guidelines for use, 5
guidelines for selection, 6

Backgrounds, design and use, 51-58, 104, 108

Balance, as design principle, 49-50

Board of trustees, as display audience, 22

Bodies, in cartoons, 85-86

Brushes, for lettering, 74, 75-76

Bulletin boards, 32-36
attachment of, 115-116
color, 115
construction, 113-117
placement of, 32, 116-117

Burlap, 12, 32, 52, 114-115

Captions
ideas for, 58-66, 69-71, 93, 94-95, 107
techniques, 73-79, 80, 120, 121

Cartoons
multi-purpose uses, 29, 34, 58-66, 93-94, 95, 101, 107, 121
techniques for executing, 65, 84-86, 93-94, 121

Cave paintings, 3

Clientele interest, as idea source, 92-93, 100-101

Clippings
posting of, 32-35, 61-62, 65
as sources of ideas, 93-94

Subject Locator

One of the purposes of this book is to show and discuss display ideas which teachers can adapt to almost any subject at any level. However, for teachers who wish to locate specific subject references, the following guide is provided.

FINE ARTS
    Arts and crafts, pages 10, 11, 13, 14, 54, 60, 88-89, 90, 91, 92. Figure 19, page 54.
    Music, pages 11, 12, 92-93, 96-97, 99-107. Figure 69, page 100; figures 75-82, pages 103 and 105.

128